SPOTLIGHT

MAINE'S SOUTHERN COAST

Including Portland

HILARY NANGLE

Contents

MAINE'S SOUTHERN COAST

SOUTHERN COAST

Drive over the I-95 bridge from New Hampshire into Maine's Southern Coast region on a bright summer day and you'll swear the air is cleaner, the sky bluer, the trees greener, the roadside signs more upbeat: Welcome to Maine: The Way Life Should Be. (*Is* it? Or maybe the way life *used* to be?)

Most visitors come to this region for the spectacular attractions of the justly world-famous Maine coast—the inlets, islands, and especially the beaches, but it's rich in history, too.

Southernmost York County, part of the Province of Maine, was incorporated in 1636 (only 16 years after the *Mayflower* pilgrims reached Plymouth, Massachusetts) and reeks of history: ancient cemeteries, musty archives, and architecturally stunning homes and public buildings. Probably the best places to dive into that history are in the sites of the Old York Historical Society in York Harbor.

Geological fortune smiled on this 50-mile ribbon, endowing it with a string of sandy beaches—nirvana for sun worshipers, less enchanting to swimmers, who need to steel themselves to spend much time in the ocean (especially in early summer, before the water temperature has reached a tolerable level).

Complementing those beaches are amusement parks and arcades, fishing shacks turned chic boutiques, a surprising number of good restaurants (given the region's seasonality), and some of the state's prettiest parks and preserves.

Spend some time poking around the small villages that give the region so much character. Many have been gussied up and gentrified

© TOM NANGLE

HIGHLIGHTS

◖ **Old York Historical Society:** York dates from the 1640s, and on this campus of historic buildings, you can peek into early life (page 19).

◖ **Nubble Light/Sohier Park:** You'll likely recognize this often-photographed Maine Coast icon, which is the easiest lighthouse to see in the region (page 19).

◖ **Ogunquit Museum of American Art (OMAA):** It's hard to say which is more jaw dropping, the art or the view (page 28).

◖ **Marginal Way:** Escape the hustle and bustle of Ogunquit with a stroll on this paved, shorefront path (page 28).

◖ **Wells Reserve at Laudholm Farm:** Orient yourself at the visitors center, where you can learn about the history, flora, and fauna, and then take a leisurely walk to the seashore, passing through a variety of habitats (page 29).

◖ **Seashore Trolley Museum:** Ring-ring-ring goes the bell...and zing-zing-zing go your heartstrings, especially if you're a trolley fan (page 40).

◖ **Dock Square:** Busy, busy, busy is this heart of Kennebunkport, and with good reason. Brave the crowds and explore (page 43).

◖ **St. Anthony's Monastery:** It's hard to believe this oasis of calm is just a short stroll from busy-busy-busy Dock Square (page 44).

LOOK FOR ◖ TO FIND RECOMMENDED SIGHTS, ACTIVITIES, DINING, AND LODGING.

◖ **East Point Sanctuary:** A must for birders, this coastal preserve provides dramatic views (page 57).

quite a bit but retain their seafaring or farming bones.

Some Mainers refer to the Southern Coast as northern Massachusetts. Sometimes it can seem that way, not only for the numbers of commonwealth plates in evidence but also because many former Massachusetts residents have moved here for the quality of life and commute to jobs in the Boston area. The downside is escalating real-estate prices that have forced families with deep roots off land that's been in their families for generations

and pushed those in traditional seafaring occupations inland. Still, if you nose around and get off the beaten path, you'll find that real Maine is still here.

PLANNING YOUR TIME

The good news is that Maine's Southern Coast is a rather compact region. The bad news is that it's heavily congested, especially in summer. Still, with a minimum of four days, you should be able to take in most of the key sights, from beaches to museums, as

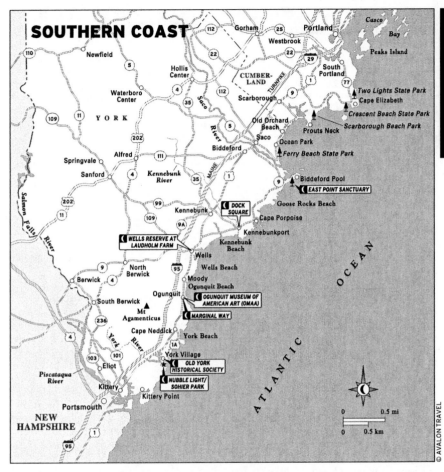

long as you don't want to spend hours basking in the sun.

Route 1, the region's primary artery, is often bumper-to-bumper traffic. If you're hopscotching towns, consider using I-95, which has exits for York, Kennebunk, and Saco/Biddeford/Old Orchard Beach. Parking, too, can be a challenge and expensive, but a trolley system operates in summer and connects most towns,

making it easy to avoid the hassles and help the environment.

July and August are the busiest months. If you can avoid them, do. Spring and fall are lovely times to visit, and most attractions are open. In winter, you can walk the beaches without running into another soul, it's easy to get dinner reservations, and lodging prices plummet—the trade-off is that fewer businesses are open.

Kittery

Besides being a natural point of entry into the state, Kittery also competes with Freeport, farther up the coast, as an outlet-shopping mecca. Kittery boasts more than 120 factory outlets lining both sides of U.S. 1. But before or after you overdose on shoes, china, tools, toys, candles, and underwear, take time to explore the back roads of Maine's oldest town—settled in 1623 and chartered in 1647. Maine is home to a lot of well-kept secrets, Kittery being one of them. Parks, a small nautical museum, historic architecture, and lobster restaurants are only a few of the attractions in Kittery and its "suburb," Kittery Point. It was also on Kittery's Badger Island where the sloop *Ranger* was launched in 1777. The shipbuilding continues at Portsmouth Naval Shipyard, on Kittery's Dennet's Island, the first government shipyard in America.

To reach Kittery's shops and services from I-95 northbound take the Exit 3 cloverleaf, designated Kittery, Coastal Route 1 North, and continue to Route 1. From I-95 southbound, take the Yorks/Berwicks exit, and then take Coastal Route 1 South. Follow signs; the twists and turns can be confusing.

SIGHTS

Avoid the outlet sprawl and see the prettiest part of the area by driving along squiggly Route 103 from the Route 1 rotary in Kittery through Kittery Point (administratively part of Kittery) and on to Route 1A in York. You can even make a day of it, stopping at the sites mentioned here. Be very careful and watch for cyclists and pedestrians, as there are no shoulders and lots of blind corners and hills.

Kittery Historical and Naval Museum

Maritime history buffs shouldn't miss the small but well-stocked Kittery Historical and Naval Museum (Rogers Road Ext., near the junction of Rtes. 1 and 236, Kittery, 207/439-3080, 10 A.M.–4 P.M. Tues.–Sat. June–mid-Oct., $3 adults, $1.50 kids 7–15, family max. $6). A

large exhibit hall and a small back room contain ship models, fishing gear, old photos and paintings, and an astonishing collection of scrimshaw (carved whale ivory).

Lady Pepperrell House

The 1760 Georgian Lady Pepperrell House (Pepperrell Rd., Rte. 103, shortly before the Fort McClary turnoff) is now privately owned and no longer open to the public, but it's worth admiring from afar. Nearby, across from the First Congregational Church, is the area's most-visited burying ground. Old-cemetery buffs should bring rubbing gear here for some interesting grave markers. The tomb of Levi Thaxter (husband of poet Celia Thaxter) bears an epitaph written for him by Robert Browning.

Fort McClary Historic Site

Since the early 18th century, fortifications have stood on this 27-acre headland, protecting Portsmouth Harbor from seaborne foes. Contemporary remnants at Fort McClary (Rte. 103, Kittery Point, 207/439-2845, $2 adults, $1 kids 5–11) are several outbuildings, an 1846 blockhouse, granite walls, and earthworks—all with a view of Portsmouth Harbor. Opposite are the sprawling buildings of the Portsmouth Naval Shipyard. Bring a picnic (covered tables and a lily pond are across the street) and turn the kids loose to run and play. It's officially open May 30–October 1, but the site is accessible in off-season. The fort is 2.5 miles east of Route 1.

Fort Foster

The only problem with Fort Foster (Pocahontas Rd., off Rte. 103, Gerrish Island, Kittery Point, 207/439-3800, 10 A.M.–8 P.M. Memorial Day–Labor Day and weekends May and Sept., $10 vehicle pass, $5 adult walk-in, $1 child walk-in) is that it's no secret, so parking can be scarce (and expensive) at this 90-acre municipal park at the entrance to Portsmouth Harbor. On a hot day, arrive early. Then you can swim, hike the nature trails, fish off the

© TOM NANGLE

Fort McClary has guarded Portsmouth Harbor since the early 18th century.

pier (no license needed), picnic, and investigate the tide pools. Bring your sailboard and a kite—there's almost always a breeze. From nearby **Seapoint Beach** (park in the small roadside lot and walk down to the beach; the lower lot is for residents only, no facilities) on a clear day, there's a wide-open view of the offshore Isles of Shoals, owned jointly by Maine and New Hampshire.

RECREATION
Brave Boat Harbor
One of the Rachel Carson National Wildlife Refuge's 10 Maine coastal segments is Brave Boat Harbor (207/646-9226), a beautifully unspoiled, 560-acre wetlands preserve in Kittery Point with a four-mile (round-trip) trail. Carry binoculars, wear rubberized boots to maneuver the squishy areas, and slather on the insect repellent. The habitat is particularly sensitive here, so be kind to the environment. Take Route 103 to Chauncey Creek Road, and continue past the Gerrish Island bridge to Cutts Island Lane. Just beyond it and across a small

bridge is a pullout on the left. You have a couple of options for hikes: a 1.8-mile loop trail, including a spur, or a half-mile loop. Bring binoculars to spot waterfowl in the marshlands.

Captain and Patty's Piscataqua River Tours
Take a spin around the Piscataqua River Basin with Captain and Patty's Piscataqua River Tours (Town Dock, Pepperrell Rd., Kittery Point, 207/439-8976 home or 207/451-8156 boat). The 80-minute historical tour departs seven times daily, including once in the evening for a two-hour twilight cruise for adults only. Along the way, Captain Neil Odams points out historic forts, lighthouses, and the Naval shipyard.

ENTERTAINMENT
Concerts in the Park
Kittery Recreation presents a free, summer concert series on Memorial Field, Old Post Road, 6:30–8 P.M. on Wednesday evenings mid-July–mid-August.

SHOPPING
No question, you'll find bargains at Kittery's 120-plus factory outlets (www.thekitteryoutlets.com)—actually a bunch of minimalls clustered along Route 1. All the household names are here: Bass, Calvin Klein, Eddie Bauer, J Crew, Mikasa, Esprit, Lenox, Timberland, Tommy Hilfiger, GAP, Villeroy and Boch, and a hundred more (all open daily). Anchoring it all is the **Kittery Trading Post** (301 Rte. 1, 207/439-2700 or 888/587-6246, www.kitterytradingpost.com), a humongous sporting-goods and clothing emporium. Try to avoid the outlets on weekends, when you might need to take a number for the try-on rooms. Most of the minimalls have telephones; several have ATMs; all have restrooms.

ACCOMMODATIONS
Put a little oooh and aaaah into your touring with a visit to the **Portsmouth Harbor Inn and Spa** (6 Water St., Kittery, 207/439-4040, www.innatportsmouth.com, $160–200

peak). The handsome brick inn, built in 1889, looks out over the Piscataqua River, Portsmouth, and the Portsmouth Naval Shipyard. Five attractive Victorian-style rooms (most with water views) are furnished with antiques and have air-conditioning, TV, and phones. There's an outdoor hot tub, and beach chairs are available. Breakfasts are multicourse feasts. Request a back room if you're noise sensitive, although air-conditioning camouflages traffic noise in summer. Rooms on the third floor have the best views, but these also have hand-held showers. Now for the aaaah part. The inn also has a full-service spa. The inn has lots of intriguing special packages. It's an easy walk across the bridge to Portsmouth for plentiful dining options.

Shopaholics take note: **Chicadee Bed and Breakfast** (63 Haley Rd., 207/439-0672 or 888/502-0876, www.chicadeebandb.net, $125 d) is within walking distance of Kittery's famed outlets. A full country breakfast should power you through a shopping spree. Afterward, return for a dip in the pool. Walter and Brenda Lawrence's family home is comfortably furnished with country flair. No pets—four dogs are in residence.

FOOD
Local Flavors

Kittery has an abundance of excellent specialty food stores that are perfect for stocking up for a picnic lunch or dinner. Most are along the section of Route 1 between the Portsmouth bridge and the traffic circle.

Three are within steps of each other. At **Beach Pea Baking Co.** (53 Rte. 1, 207/439-3555, 7:30 A.M.–6 P.M. Mon.–Sat.) you can buy fabulous breads and pastries. Sandwiches and salads are made to order 11 A.M.–3 P.M. daily. There's pleasant seating indoors and on a patio. Next door is **Golden Harvest** (7 A.M.–6:30 P.M. Mon.–Sat. and 9 A.M.–6 P.M. Sun.), where you can load up on luscious produce. Across the street is **Terracotta Pasta Co.** (52A, Rte. 1, 207/475-3025, 10 A.M.– 6 P.M. Mon., 9 A.M.–6:30 P.M. Tues.–Sat., and noon–4 P.M. Sun.), where in addition

to handmade pastas you'll find salads, soups, sandwiches, prepared foods, and lots of other goodies.

Just off Route 1 is **Enoteca Italiana** (20 Walker St., 207/439-7216, 10 A.M.–7 P.M. Mon. and Wed.–Sat. and noon–4 P.M. Sun.), which carries wine, an extensive selection of cured meats, fine cheeses, and other gourmet items.

What's a meal without chocolate? At **Cacao** (64 Government St., just off the town green, 207/438-9001, noon–6 P.M. Tues.–Fri. and 10 A.M.–4 P.M. Sat.), Susan Tuveson handcrafts outrageously decadent chocolate truffles and caramels. Flavors vary from the familiar to the exotic: Some are made with chilies (habanero lime!), some with cheeses. The strawberry balsamic vinegar with black pepper truffle and the fleur de sel caramel are particularly sublime.

Old World artisan breads made from organic ingredients are available at the company store for **When Pigs Fly** (447 Rte. 1, 207/439-3114, www.sendbread.com).

In Kittery Point, **Frisbee's Supermarket** (207/439-0014, 7 A.M.–8 P.M. Mon.–Sat., 8 A.M.–8 P.M. Sun.) is an experience in itself. Established in 1828, the store has marginally modernized but still earns its label as North America's oldest family store—run by the fifth generation of Frisbees.

At the **Sunrise Grill** (182 State Rd., Rte. 1, Kittery Traffic Circle, Kittery, 207/439-5748, 6:30 A.M.–2 P.M. daily), order waffles, granola, omelettes, or Diana's Benedict or at lunch, salads, sandwiches, and burgers. In downtown Kittery, **Crooked Lane Café** (Wentworth St., 207/439-2244), in a Victorian building with a tin ceiling and both indoor and outdoor seating, is a bit more polished and serves a full menu of espresso-style coffees along with breakfast and lunch fare.

Craving Mex? Some of the recipes in Luis Valdez's **Loco Coco's Tacos** (36 Walker St., Kittery, 207/438-9322, www.locococos.com, 11 A.M.–3 P.M. and 4–8 P.M. Mon.–Fri., to 9 P.M. Sat.) have been passed down for generations, and the homemade salsas are fab. If you're feeling really decadent, go for the artery-busting California fries. There's a kids' menu, too. Nothing costs more than $9.

Casual Dining

Dining in Kittery took a bit of an upswing with the opening of **anneke jans** (60 Wallingford Sq., Kittery, 207/439-0001, www.annekejans.net, 5–10 P.M. Tues.–Sat.). Charcoal walls, white-clothed tables with moss centerpieces, a wine bar, and windows that open to the street create an especially hip and stylin' atmosphere. The French/American bistro menu might include blue-corn-dusted sea scallops, herb-roasted chicken, or Angus strip sirloin, with prices ranging $14–31. The extensive wine list has more than 30 available by the glass. This is a local hot spot with a lively crowd; reservations are recommended.

Lobster and Clams

If you came to Maine to eat lobster, **Chauncey Creek Lobster Pier** (16 Chauncey Creek Rd., off Rte. 103, Kittery Point, 207/439-1030, www.chaunceycreek.com, 11 A.M.–8 P.M., to 7 P.M. after Labor Day, mid-May–Columbus Day) is the real deal. Step up to the window, place your order, take a number, and grab a table (you may need to share) overlooking tidal Chauncey Creek and the woods on the close-in opposite shore. It's a particularly picturesque—and extremely popular—place. Parking is a nightmare. BYOB and anything else that's not on the menu.

If clams are high on your must-have list, you can't do much better than **Bob's Clam Hut** (315 Rte. 1, Kittery 03904, 207/439-4233, www.bobsclamhut.com, 11 A.M.–9 P.M. Mon.–Thurs., to 9:30 P.M. Fri. and Sat., to 8:30 P.M. Sun.), next to the Kittery Trading Post. Using vegetable oil for frying, Bob's turns out everything from scallops to shrimp to calamari to, of course, clams—the tartar sauce is the secret weapon. Expect to pay market rates, but nothing is too pricey. Bob's is open all year.

The Berwicks

Probably the best known of the area's present-day inland communities is the riverside town of South Berwick—thanks to a historical and literary tradition dating to the 17th century, and antique cemeteries to prove it. The 19th- and 20th-century novels of Sarah Orne Jewett and Gladys Hasty Carroll have lured many a contemporary visitor to explore their rural settings—an area aptly described by Carroll as "a small patch of earth continually occupied but never crowded for more than three hundred years."

Also here is the 150-acre hilltop campus of **Berwick Academy,** Maine's oldest prep school, chartered in 1791 with John Hancock's signature. The coed school's handsome gray-stone William H. Fogg Memorial Library ("The Fogg") is named for the same family connected with Harvard's Fogg Art Museum. The highlight of the library is an incredible collection of dozens of 19th-century stained-glass windows, most designed by Victorian artist Sarah Wyman Whitman, who also designed jackets for Sarah Orne Jewett's books. Thanks to a diligent fund-raising effort, the windows were recently restored to their former glory.

SIGHTS
Sarah Orne Jewett House

Don't blink or you might miss the tiny sign outside the 1774 Sarah Orne Jewett House (5 Portland St., Rtes. 4 and 236, South Berwick, 207/384-2454, www.historicnewengland.org, 11 A.M.–5 P.M. Fri.–Sun. June 1–Oct. 15, $8 adults, $7 seniors, $4 ages 12 and younger) smack in the center of town. Park on the street and join one of the tours—you'll learn details of the Jewett family and its star, Sarah (1849–1909), author of *The Country of the Pointed Firs,* a New England classic. Books by and about Sarah are

Author Sarah Orne Jewett made her home in South Berwick.

available in the gift shop. House tours are at 11 A.M. and 1, 2, 3, and 4 P.M. The house is a Historic New England property.

Hamilton House

Dramatically crowning a bluff overlooking the Salmon Falls River and flanked by handsome colonial revival gardens, 18th-century Hamilton House (40 Vaughan's La., South Berwick, 207/384-2454, www.historicnewengland.org, 11 A.M.–5 P.M. Wed.–Sun. June 1–Oct. 15, $8 adults, $7 seniors, $4 ages 12 and younger) evokes history and tradition. Like the Jewett House, the 35-acre site is owned by Historic New England. Knowledgeable guides relate the house's fascinating history. Tours begin only on the hour—last one at 4 P.M. In July, the **Sunday in the Garden** concert series takes place on the lawn ($8 admission, including a free pass to come back and see the house). Pray for sun; the concert is moved indoors on rainy days. From Route 236 at the southern edge of South Berwick (watch for a signpost), turn left onto Brattle Street and take the second right onto Vaughan's Lane.

Vaughan Woods State Park

A path connects Hamilton House to adjoining Vaughan Woods State Park (28 Oldfields Rd., South Berwick, 207/384-5160, 9 A.M.–8 P.M. late May–early Sept., but accessible all year, $2 adults, $1 children 5–11, free over 65 or under 5), but it's not easy to find, and there's much more parking space at the main entrance to the 250-acre river's-edge preserve. Three miles of maintained trails wind through this underused park, and benches are scattered here and there. There's even a bench looking out over the river and Hamilton House.

Old Berwick Historical Society/ Counting House

Based in a onetime cotton-mill building known as the Counting House, the Old Berwick Historical Society (Liberty and Main Sts., Rte. 4, P.O. Box 296, South Berwick 03908, 207/384-0000, www.obhs.net, 1–4 P.M. Sat.–Sun. in July, Aug., and Sept.,), sees a steady stream of genealogists looking for their roots in one of Maine's oldest settlements. Books and documents are only part of the museum's collection, which includes old photos and tools, boat models and nautical instruments, plus special annual exhibits. Admission to the 19th-century Counting House is by donation.

ENTERTAINMENT

Theatergoers head to the Berwick area for the long-running (since 1972) **Hackmatack Playhouse** (538 School St./Rte. 9, Berwick, 207/698-1807, www.hackmatack.org), midway between North Berwick and Berwick. The popular summer theater, based in a renovated barn reminiscent of a past era, has 8 P.M. performances (comedies and musical comedies) Wednesday–Saturday and a 2 P.M. matinee Thursday. The ambience is relaxed and casual but quality is high, though it's a non-Equity house. The Hackmatack season runs late June–early September. Tickets are $20; discounts for seniors and students except Saturday.

ACCOMMODATIONS

Once the headmaster's residence for nearby Berwick Academy, the elegant, turn-of-the-20th-century **Academy Street Inn Bed and Breakfast** (15 Academy St., South Berwick, 207/384-5633) has crystal chandeliers, leaded-glass windows, working fireplaces, and high-ceilinged rooms full of antiques. Paul and Lee Fopeano's handsome home has five rooms with private baths ($84–94 d). Full breakfast

or afternoon lemonade on the 60-foot screened porch is a real treat. It's open all year.

FOOD

A local institution since 1960, **Fogarty's** (471 Main St., South Berwick, 207/384-8361, 11 A.M.–8 P.M., to 9 P.M. Sat.) has expanded through the years from a simple takeout to a local favorite for inexpensive, family-friendly dining. Ask for a river-view table in the back room.

Newer on the scene is **Pepperland Café** (279 Main St., South Berwick, 207/384-5535, 11 A.M.–11:30 P.M. Tues.–Sat., 9 A.M.–3 P.M. Sun.), a family-friendly pub-meets-bistro serving comfort food with pizzazz. Make a meal from smaller plates and salads ($5–10) or go big with the entrées ($16–19). Everything's prepared from scratch, and more than half of the waste is recycled.

Now here's a find: a cozy French bistro serving simple yet classic fare created from farm-fresh ingredients. **Margaux: Bistro Populaire** (404 Main St., South Berwick, 207/384-8249, 5:30–9 P.M. Tues.–Sat.) is an intimate, low-key neighborhood bistro, where Linda Robinson and Christine Prunier provide a warm welcome into the simple white house, with dining on the enclosed porch, one small dining room, and at the small bar. The frequently changing menu might include escargot au Pernod, braised lamb shank, duck confit, or seared sea scallops. Mix and match from small and large plates. Entrée range is $18–25.

The Yorks

Four villages with distinct personalities—upscale York Harbor, historic York Village, casual York Beach, and semirural Cape Neddick—make up the Town of York. First inhabited by Native Americans, who named it Agamenticus, the area was settled as early as 1624—so history is serious business here. Town high points were its founding, by Sir Ferdinando Gorges, and the arrival of well-to-do vacationers in the 19th century. In between were Indian massacres,

economic woes, and population shuffles. The town's winter population explodes in summer (pretty obvious in July and August, when you're searching for a free patch of York Beach sand or a parking place). York Beach, with its seasonal surf and souvenir shops and amusements, has long been the counterpoint to genteel York Village, but that's changing with the restoration and rebirth of downtown buildings and the arrival of tony restaurants, shops, and condos.

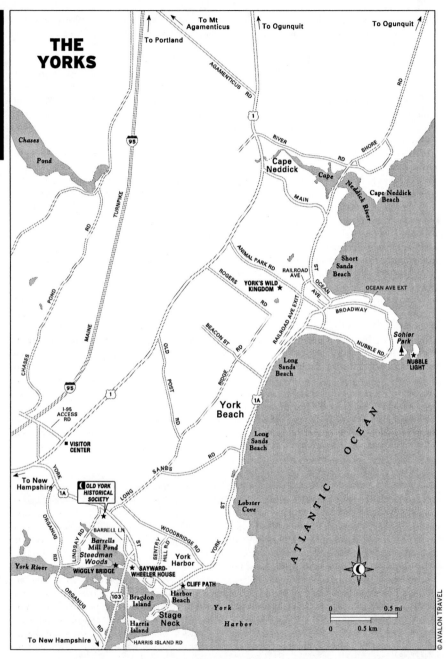

History and genealogy buffs can study the headstones in the Old Burying Ground or comb the archives of the Old York Historical Society. For lighthouse fans, there are Cape Neddick Light Station ("Nubble Light") and, six miles offshore, Boon Island. You can rent horses or mountain bikes on Mt. Agamenticus, board a deep-sea fishing boat in York Harbor, or spend an hour hiking the Cliff Path in York Harbor. For the kids, there's a zoo, a lobster-boat cruise, a taffy maker, or, of course, back to the beach.

SIGHTS
◖ Old York Historical Society
Based in York Village, the Old York Historical Society (207 York St., P.O. Box 312, York 03909, 207/363-4974, www.oldyork.org, museum buildings open 10 A.M.–5 P.M. Mon.–Sat. early June–early Oct., $10 adults or $5 one building, $8 seniors or $4 one building, $5 children 4–16 or $3 one building) is the driving force behind a collection of eight colonial and postcolonial buildings (plus a research library) open throughout the summer. Start at the Jefferds' Tavern Visitor Center (5 Lindsay Rd., York), where you'll need to pick up tickets for visiting. Don't miss the Old Burying Ground, dating from 1735, across the street (rubbings are a no-no). Nearby are the Old Gaol and the School House (both fun for kids), Ramsdell House, and the Emerson-Wilcox House. About one-half mile down Lindsay Road, on the York River, are the John Hancock Warehouse and the George Marshall Store Gallery (140 Lindsay Rd., operated in the summer as a respected contemporary-art gallery); across the river is the Elizabeth Perkins House. Antiques buffs shouldn't miss the Wilcox and Perkins Houses. These two are open by guided tour; other buildings are self guided. Visit some or all of the buildings, at your own pace—no one leads you from one to another. In July and August, an architectural walking tour of York Village begins at 10 A.M. every Wednesday ($2 pp; meet at Jefferds' Tavern). At 196 York Street, across from the jail, is the well-stocked Museum Shop. Note: Some sites you can walk

to from the tavern; others you'll need a car to reach and parking may be limited.

◖ Nubble Light/Sohier Park
The best-known photo op in York is the distinctive 1879 lighthouse known formally as Cape Neddick Light Station and familiarly as "The Nubble." Although there's no access to the lighthouse's island, Sohier Park Welcome Center (Nubble Rd., off Rte. 1A, between Long and Short Sands Beaches, York Beach, 207/363-7608, 10 A.M.–8 P.M. daily June–mid-Sept. and weekends in May and to early Oct.) provides the perfect viewpoint (and has restrooms). Parking is limited, but the turnover is fairly good. Not a bad idea, however, to walk from the Long Sands parking area or come by bike, even though the road has inadequate shoulders. Weekdays this is also a popular spot for scuba divers.

Sayward-Wheeler House
Owned by the Boston-based Historic New England, the 1718 Sayward-Wheeler House (9 Barrell La. Ext., York Harbor, 207/384-2454, www.historicnewengland.org, $5) occupies a prime site at the edge of York Harbor. It's open with tours on the hour 11 A.M.–4 P.M. the first and third Saturday of the month, from June through mid-October. In the house are lots of period furnishings—all in pristine condition. Take Route 1A to Lilac Lane (Rte. 103) to Barrell Lane and then to Barrell Lane Extension.

York's Wild Kingdom
More than 250 creatures—including tigers, zebras, llamas, deer, lions, elephants, and monkeys—find a home at York's Wild Kingdom (102 Railroad Ave., off Rte. 1, York Beach, 207/363-4911 or 800/456-4911, www.yorkzoo.com). It's not what you'd call a state-of-the-art zoo, but it keeps the kids entertained. Elephant shows and other animal "events" occur three times daily in July and August—usually at noon, 2 P.M., and 4 P.M., but the schedule is posted, or you can call ahead. Between the zoo and the amusement-

SOUTHERN COAST LIGHTHOUSE TOUR

The lure of lighthouses is understandable. Legends tell of heroic keepers, prank-playing ghosts, and death-defying storms. Lighthouse lovers will find five in southern Maine, all viewable (binoculars will help) from land. Most of these were built in the 19th century on the wrecks of earlier lights that couldn't withstand winter storms.

Begin your journey by taking Route 103, off Route 1 in Kittery, and heading north. The best place to view **Whaleback Lighthouse,** which guards the Portsmouth Harbor and the mouth of the Piscataqua River, is from Fort Foster, on Gerrish Island, which is connected to the mainland via a bridge.

Continue on Route 103 until it merges with Route 1A, and then follow this north, bearing right, at the end of Long Sands Beach, on Nubble Road. The Cape Neddick Light, better known as **The Nubble,** stands just 200 yards or so off Cape Neddick Point and is easily seen from Sohier Park.

Sohier Park is also the best place to view the **Boon Island Light,** six miles offshore. The first three lighthouses constructed on this remote pile of rock were destroyed before the current light, dating from the mid-19th century, was constructed of hand-hewn granite blocks.

Continue on 1A until it joins Route 1, and then head north. Break from viewing real lighthouses for a visit to the king of lighthouse emporia, **Lighthouse Depot,** on Route 1 in Wells.

After touring, browsing, buying, and learning everything there is to know about lighthouses, continue north on Route 1 until Route 9 East splits from it, just north of Wells. Follow Route 9 through the Kennebunks and on to the village of Cape Porpoise. The town pier, at the end of Pier Road, is the best place to view the **Goat Island Lighthouse,** which has the distinction of being the last manned lighthouse in the state. It was finally automated in 1990. There's also a great view from the Vaughn's Island Preserve, in Kennebunkport, but you'll have coordinate your visit with the tide.

Return to Route 9, and continue east until it merges with Route 208. You'll turn right, following signs for Biddeford Pool. The **Wood Island Lighthouse,** on the east end of Wood Island, marks the entrance to the Saco River. It can be seen from several points in Biddeford Pool and Hills Beach, but the best view is from the East Point Audubon Sanctuary.

---

park rides, it's easy to spend a day here—and there are snack bars on the grounds. Admission (covering the zoo and some of the rides) is in the neighborhood of $18 adults, $15 children 4–10, $4 age 3 and younger. Zoo-only admission is $14 adults, $9 or $1 kids. The zoo's open 10 A.M.–5 P.M., to 6 P.M. weekends and July and August, from late May to late September; amusement park hours are noon–9:30 P.M. late June through early September.

Spooky Sightseeing

Flickering candles and a black-hooded guide get you right in the spirit of things during imaginative evening candlelight walking tours of historic York village. **Ghostly Tours** (250 York St., Rte. 1A, York, 207/363-0000, www.ghostlytours.com) specializes in ghost stories and 18th-century folklore during its 45-minute meanders through burial grounds in the oldest part of town. (Even the phone number is kinda weird.) Cost is $10 pp. To continue the theme, **Gravestone Artwear** (same address, 207/351-1434 or 800/564-4310) carries wizard capes, gravestone rubbing kits (but don't try them out in the Old Burying Ground), notecards, T-shirts, and lots of other cemetery-centered items.

RECREATION
Walk the Walks

Next to Harbor Beach, near the Stage Neck Inn, a sign marks the beginning of the **Cliff Path,** a walkway worth taking for its dramatic harbor views in the shadow of elegant summer cottages. On the one-hour round-trip, you'll

© TOM NANGLE

The Wiggly Bridge leads to Steedman Woods preserve.

pass the York Harbor Reading Room (an exclusive club). The path is on private property, traditionally open to the public courtesy of the owners, but controversy surfaces periodically about property rights, vandalism, and the condition of some sections of the walk. Note: It's called the Cliff Path for a reason. It's not a good choice for little ones.

A less strenuous route is known variously as the **Shore Path, Harbor Walk,** or **Fisherman's Walk,** running west along the harbor and river from Stage Neck Road (next to Edwards' Harborside Inn) and passing the Sayward-Wheeler House before crossing the tiny, green-painted Wiggly Bridge leading into the **Steedman Woods** preserve. Carry binoculars for good boat watching and birding in the 16-acre preserve, owned by the Old York Historical Society. A one-mile double-loop trail takes less than an hour of easy strolling.

Mt. Agamenticus

Drive to the summit of Mt. Agamenticus ("The

Big A") and you're at York County's highest point. It's only 692 feet, but on a clear day you'll have panoramic views of ocean, lakes, woods, and sometimes the White Mountains. The preserve, comprising 7,000 acres of conservation land and 4,500 acres of water district land, is considered among the most biologically diverse wildernesses in Maine, and its landscape includes vernal pools and ponds and it's home to rare and endangered species. At the top are a billboard map of the 40-mile trail network and a curious memorial to St. Aspinquid, a 17th-century Algonquian Indian leader. Also here are riding stables, offering trail rides Memorial Day to mid-September. Mountain biking is also hugely popular on Agamenticus. Take a picnic, a kite, and binoculars. In the fall, if the wind's from the northwest, watch for migrating hawks; in winter, bring a sled for the best downhill run in southern Maine. Contact the **York Parks and Recreation Department** (207/363-1040) for info about the trail rides and other activities at the mountain park. Fortunately, in recent years, conservationists have been particularly active here, saving thousands of acres from development. The efforts continue, with a goal of 14,000 acres. From Route 1 in Cape Neddick, take Mountain Road (also called Agamenticus Rd.) 4.2 miles west to the access road.

Golf

The **Ledges Golf Club** (1 Ledges Dr., off Rte. 91, York, 207/351-9999, www.ledges-golf.com) is an 18-hole course with daily public tee times.

Swimming

Sunbathing and swimming are big draws in York, with four beaches of varying sizes and accessibility. Bear in mind that traffic can be gridlocked along the beachfront (Rte. 1A) in midsummer, so it may take longer than you expect to get anywhere. **Lifeguards** are on duty 9:30 A.M.–4 P.M. mid-June–Labor Day at Short Sands Beach, Long Beach, and Harbor Beach. Bathhouses at Long Sands and Short Sands are open 9 A.M.–7 P.M. daily in midsummer. The biggest parking space (metered) is at Long Sands, but that 1.5-mile beach also draws the most customers. Scarcest parking is at Harbor Beach, near the Stage Neck Inn, and at Cape Neddick (Passaconaway) Beach, near the Ogunquit town line.

Sea Kayaking

Kayak rentals are available for $30 a day, single, $45 double, from **Excursions: Coastal Maine Outfitting Company** (1399 Rte. 1, Cape Neddick, 207/363-0181, www.excursionsinmaine.com), owned by Mike Sullivan and Scott Leighton. Or sign up for one of their half-day tours: $55 (afternoon) or $60 (morning, with lunch). Kids 10–15 are $5 less. A four-hour basics clinic for ages 16 and older is $75; another for those comfortable with basics is also $75. Sea-kayak rental is $30/day or $45 for 24-hour period per double, $45/$60 for a single. Excursions is on Route 1 four miles north of the I-95 York exit.

Harbor Adventures (Harris Island Rd., York Harbor, 207/363-8466, www.harboradventures.com) offers instruction and guided sea-kayaking trips from Kittery through Kennebunkport. Prices begin around $40 for a two-hour harbor tour.

Scuba and Surfing

York Beach Scuba (19 Railroad Ave., P.O. Box 850, York Beach 03910, 207/363-3330), a source for rentals, air, and trips, is conveniently situated not far from Sohier Park, a popular dive site. It also offers diving packages, including lodging and meals. For surfing information, lessons, or rentals, call **Liquid Dreams Surf Shop** (171 Long Beach Ave., York, 207/351-2545). It's open 10 A.M.–5 P.M. weekends, and it's right across from the beach.

Fishing

Local expert on fly-fishing, spin fishing, and conventional tackle is **Eldgrege Bros. Guide Service** (1480 Rte. 1, Cape Neddick, 207/373-9269, www.eldredgeflyshop.com). Four-hour guided trips for one or two anglers begin at $250 freshwater, $300

salt water. Kayak and rod and reel rentals are available.

ENTERTAINMENT
Live Music

Inn on the Blues (7 Ocean Ave., York Beach, 207/351-3221, www.innontheblues.com) has live music (acoustic, blues, reggae) every night but Monday during the summer. If you want to be close to both the music and the beach, consider booking one of the suites upstairs ($155–390).

The **Ship's Cellar Pub** in the York Harbor Inn frequently has live entertainment, too.

Free concerts are often held at the **Ellis Park Gazebo,** usually 7–9 P.M. from early July to early September.

FESTIVALS AND EVENTS

Each year, the Old York Historical Society invites decorators to transform a local house for the **Decorator Show House,** culminating in an open house from mid-July to mid-August.

From late July into early August, the **York Days** festivities enliven the town for 10 days with concerts, dances, walking tours, a road race, sandcastle contests, antiques and art shows, a dog show, fireworks, a parade, and public suppers.

York Village's **Annual Harvestfest** takes place 10 A.M.–4 P.M. the weekend after Columbus Day in October and combines colonial crafts and cooking demonstrations, hayrides, museum tours, entertainment for adults and kids, and an ox roast with beanhole beans. This is one of the town's most popular events; most activities are free.

The annual **Lighting of the Nubble,** in late November, includes cookies, hot chocolate, music, and an appearance by Santa Claus. The best part, though, is seeing the lighthouse glowing for the holidays.

SHOPPING

Park in York Village and wander around the handful of small shops. **York Village Marketplace** (211 York St., Rte. 1A, York Village, 207/363-4830) is a three-level emporium based in a restored 1834 church. Lots of tasteful stuff, with an emphasis on antiques—bet you won't leave empty-handed. A model train shop occupies the entire third floor—go just to see the elaborate model set up in the shop.

Expect to wash your hands before examining any of the 400-plus, museum-quality antique quilts at Betsy Telford's **Rocky Mountain Quilts** (130 York St., York Village, 207/363-6800 or 800/762-5940, www.rockymountainquilts.com). This isn't a place for browsers.

Fans of fine craft shouldn't miss **Panache** (1949 Rte. 1, Cape Neddick, 207/646-4878). It boasts of having New England's largest selection of fine contemporary art glass, but there's so much more here. It's a visual treat. Find it just south of the Ogunquit Playhouse, on the York-Ogunquit town line.

ACCOMMODATIONS
York Harbor

Bed-and-Breakfasts: Hosts Donna and Paul Archibald have turned Fannie Chapman's 1889 summer cottage into the elegant and romantic **C Chapman Cottage** (370 York St., P.O. Box 575, York Harbor 03911, 207/363-2059 or 877/363-2059, www.chapmancottagebandb.com, $155–250), a truly special retreat. Rooms are huge and plush, with air-conditioning, Wi-Fi, TV, and spacious baths; most have whirlpool baths and fireplaces (some in the bathrooms), and a few have private decks and river views. The pampering includes a welcome fruit basket, fresh flowers, bathrobes, and fine linens. The inn also has a lovely dining room and an inviting lounge with tapas menu and martini/wine bar.

Inviting Adirondack-style chairs accent the green lawn rolling down to the harbor at **Edwards' Harborside Inn** (7 Stage Neck Rd., P.O. Box 866, York Harbor 03911, 207/363-3037 or 800/273-2686, www.edwardsharborside.com, $150–220 rooms, $150–320 suites). Many of the 10 rooms can be combined into suites, and most have water views. All have TV, phone, and air-conditioning. One suite has a party-size whirlpool tub facing the harbor, another a grand piano. Watch the sunset

from the inn's 210-foot pier, stroll the adjacent shorefront paths, wander over to the beach, or just settle into one of those shorefront chairs and watch the world go by. A full lovely buffet breakfast is served in the water-view sunporch.

Bill and Bonney Alstrom, former innkeepers at Tanglewood Hall, weren't looking to downsize, but on a lark, they stumbled upon this woodland cottage, and they were smitten. After more than a year of renovations, they opened **Morning Glory Inn** (120 Seabury Rd., York, 207/363-2062, www.morninggloryinnmaine.com, $155–225 peak). A boutique B&B, catering to romantics, the Morning Glory has just three rooms, all very spacious and private, and all with doors to private patios or yards, air-conditioning, TV with DVD, fridge, Wi-Fi, and plentiful other little amenities. The living room, in the original section of the house, was a 17th-century cottage, barged over from the Isle of Shoals; the newer post-and-beam great room doubles as a dining area, where a hot breakfast buffet is served. The property is ultraquiet—listen to the birds singing in the gardens; it's truly a magical setting, far removed yet convenient to everything York offers.

Full-Service Inns: York Harbor Inn (Rte. 1A, P.O. Box 573, York Harbor 03911, 207/363-5119 or 800/343-3869, www.yorkharborinn.com, $99–349 d) is an accommodating in-town spot with a country-inn flavor and a wide variety of room and package-plan options throughout the year. The oldest section of the inn is a 17th-century cabin from the Isles of Shoals. Accommodations are spread out in the inn, adjacent Yorkshire building, and two elegantly restored houses, both with resident innkeepers: neighboring Harbor Hill, and 1730 Harbor Crest, about a half mile away. All have TV, phones, free Wi-Fi, and air-conditioning; some have four-poster beds, fireplaces, and whirlpools; many have water views. Rates include a generous continental breakfast.

You can't miss the **Stage Neck Inn** (100 Stage Neck Rd., P.O. Box 70, York Harbor 03911, 207/363-3850 or 800/340-9901, www.stageneck.com), occupying its own private peninsula overlooking York Harbor. Modern, resort-style facilities include two pools (one indoors), tennis courts, golf privileges, fitness center, and spectacular views from balconies and terraces. The formal Harbor Porches restaurant (no jeans; entrées $21–30) and the casual Sandpiper Bar and Grille are open to the public. Peak-season rates are $235–345 d mid-May–Labor Day (special packages and MAP are available). Open all year.

York Beach

Hotel and Motel: For more than 150 years, **The Union Bluff** (8 Beach St., P.O. Box 1860, York Beach 03910, 207/363-1333 or 800/833-0721, www.unionbluff.com, $159–329 peak) has stood sentry, like a fortress, overlooking Short Sands Beach. Many of the rooms have ocean views. All have TV, air-conditioning, and phone; some have fireplace, whirlpool bath, or ocean-view deck. Furnishings are modern motel-style. Also on the premises are the Beach Street Grill dining room and a pub serving lighter fare. Best deals are the packages, which include breakfast and dinner. The hotel and pub are open year-round; the restaurant is seasonal.

Bed-and-Breakfasts: Everything's casual and flowers are everywhere at the brightly painted **Katahdin Inn** (11 Ocean Ave. Ext., P.O. Box 193, York Beach 03910, 207/363-1824, www.thekatahdininn.com, $65–125 d), overlooking the breakers of Short Sands Beach. Longtime owners Rae and Paul LeBlanc appropriately refer to it as a "bed and beach." It was built in 1863 and has always been a guesthouse. Nine smallish first-, second-, and third-floor rooms (eight with water views) have lots of four-poster beds and mostly shared baths. Breakfast is not included, but coffee is always available, the rooms have refrigerators, and several eateries are nearby. It's open mid-May–October.

Not oceanfront, but offering ocean views from many rooms and just a short walk from Short Sands Beach, is Barbara and Michael Sheff's **Candleshop Inn** (44 Freeman St., P.O. Box 1216, York Beach 03910,

207/363-4087 or 888/363-4087, www.candleshopinn.com, $110–170 peak). The 10 guest rooms (private and shared baths) are decorated in a country cottage style, with area rugs, painted furniture, and florals; many are set up for families. The day begins with a vegetarian breakfast and a stretch-and-relaxation class. Spa services, including massage and Reiki, are available on-site by appointment.

Condominium Suites: Fabulously sited on the oceanfront and overlooking the Nubble Light, the high-end **ViewPoint** (229 Nubble Rd., York Beach, 207/363-2661, www.viewpointhotel.com, $295 one bedroom–$575 three bedroom per night, $2,100–3,695 per week) comprises luxuriously appointed one-, two-, and three-bedroom suites. All have gas fireplace, fully equipped kitchen, washer/dryer, TV/VCR, phone, private patio, porch, or deck, Wi-Fi, and daily maid service. On the premises are an outdoor heated pool, grilling area, gardens, and playground.

Cape Neddick

A convenient location is the biggest selling point for the **Country View Motel and Guesthouse** (1521 Rte. 1, Cape Neddick, 207/363-7260 or 800/258-6598, www.countryviewmotel.com, $89–220 peak), a well-cared-for property with a variety of accommodations. Motel rooms vary from standard to ones with full kitchens; those in the 18th-century guesthouse have more of a B&B flair; all have air-conditioning, phone, and TV. On the premises are a pool and a picnic area with gas grills. Rates include continental breakfast. Pets are permitted in the motel.

Seasonal Rentals

Several companies manage week- or month-long rental properties, usually houses or condos. Weekly rentals begin and end on Saturday. Best is **Seaside Vacation Rentals** (Meadowbrook Plaza, 647 Rte. 1, P.O. Box 2000, York 03909, 207/363-1825, www.seasiderentals.com), a longtime family-operated firm with more than 500 properties in York, Ogunquit, Wells, Kennebunk, and Kittery.

© TOM NANGLE

Cape Neddick Light Station is locally known as "The Nubble."

CAMPING

Dixon's Coastal Maine Campground (1740 Rte. 1, Cape Neddick, 207/363-3626, www .dixonscampground.com, $30–36) has more than 100 well-spaced sites on 40 wooded and open acres. It can accommodate tents and small RVs. Electric and water hookups are available. Facilities include a playground and a good-size outdoor heated pool. It's also the base for Excursions Sea Kayaking.

FOOD
Seacoast Fine Dining Club

More than two dozen restaurants on Maine's Southern Coast participate in the Seacoast Fine Dining Club (P.O. Box 228, Newmarket, NH 03857, 603/292-5093, www.seacoastfinedining.com). Membership costs $29.95 and entitles you to buy one entrée and get a second one of equal or lesser value free. It also provides discounts on some area attractions.

Local Flavors

Both *Gourmet* and *Saveur* know where to get

dogs. Sometimes the line runs right out the door of the low-ceilinged, reddish-brown roadside shack that houses local institution **Flo's Steamed Dogs** (Rte. 1, opposite the Mountain Rd. turnoff, Cape Neddick). Founder Flo Stacy died at age 92 in June 2000, but her legend and her family live on. No menu here—just steamed Schultz wieners, buns, chips, beverages, and an attitude. The secret? The spicy, sweet-sour hot-dog sauce (allegedly once sought by the H. J. Heinz corporation, but the proprietary Stacy family isn't telling or selling). The cognoscenti know to order their dogs only with mayonnaise and the special sauce—nothing heretical such as catsup or mustard. It's open all year, 11 A.M.–3 P.M., and not a minute later, Thursday–Tuesday. Flo's has added stands in Kittery, Sanford, and Wells.

See those people with their faces pressed to the glass? They're all watching the taffy makers inside **The Goldenrod** (2 Railroad Ave., York Beach, 207/363-2621), where machines spew out 180 Goldenrod Kisses a minute, 65 tons a year—and have been at it since 1896. (The shop also accepts mail orders.) The Goldenrod is an old-fashioned place, with a tearoom, gift shop, old-fashioned soda fountain (135 ice-cream flavors), and casual dining room, with equally old-fashioned prices. It's open for breakfast (8 A.M.), lunch, and dinner daily late May–Columbus Day.

Tucked behind the York County Federal Credit Union is a delicious find, **Food and Co.** (1 York St./Rte. 1, York, 207/363-0900, www.foodnco.com, 7 A.M.–7 P.M. Mon.–Sat.). The combination gourmet food store and café does everything right: breakfast, lunch, and dinners to go (order by 3 P.M. and pick up after 5 P.M.). Prices are reasonable—most breakfast and lunch items are around $7—and the flavors creative and divine.

The *best* pies and other goodies come from **Pie in the Sky Bakery** (corner of Rte. 1 and River Rd., Cape Neddick, 207/363-2656, www.pieintheskymaine.com, 9 A.M.–6 P.M. Fri.–Mon.). You can pick up a slice for $4.50 or the whole pie for $25. Possibilities are numerous: apple crumb, blueberry, bumbleberry, jumbleberry, peach raspberry, and so on; all are handcrafted and made without preservatives or trans fats.

After viewing The Nubble, head across the road to **Brown's Ice Cream** (232 Nubble Rd., York Beach, 207/363-1277), where unusual flavors complement the standards.

Stop in at the **Gateway Farmers Market** (York Chamber of Commerce Visitor Center, Rte. 1, York, 9 A.M.–noon Sat., mid-June–mid-Oct.) and stock up for a picnic. If you still need more, head next door to Stonewall Kitchen.

Good Eats

The York Harbor Inn's **Ship's Cellar Pub** (11:30 A.M.–12:30 A.M. Mon.–Sat. and 4 P.M.–midnight Sun.) attracts even the locals. On the menu are soups, sandwiches, and salads as well as heftier entrées ($16–31), such as chicken scalopinne and pan lobster supreme. The food's good; the service is so-so. The pub doubles as a favorite local watering hole, with live music Wednesday–Sunday. Happy hour, with free

munchies, is 4–6 P.M. and sometimes draws a raucous crowd.

Wood-fired pizza and finger-licking ribs are the best sellers at **Ruby's Genuine Wood Grill** (433 Rte. 1, a mile south of the I-95 exit, York, 207/363-7980, www.rubysgrill.com, 11:30 A.M.–10 P.M., to 11 P.M. Fri. and Sat.), but there's plenty more on the menu. Some of the pizzas are downright intriguing—pulled pork and barbecue sauce, for instance. Entrées vary from St. Louis ribs to fajitas to mahimahi, most priced in the low teens. Pastas, sandwiches, salads, and burgers fill out the menu. Lots of variety and flair here. In nice weather, opt for the enclosed deck, where there's often live music Saturday night.

Wild Willy's (765 Rte. 1, York, 207/3363-9924, www.wildwillysburgers.com, 11 A.M.–8 P.M. Mon.–Sat.) has turned burgers into an art form. More than a dozen hefty, mouthwatering burgers, all made from certified Angus beef, are available, from the classic Willy burger to the Rio Grande, with roasted green chiles from New Mexico and cheddar cheese. Don't miss the hand-cut fries. Chicken sandwiches, steak chili, and frappes are also served, as are beer and wine. Order at the counter before grabbing a seat in the dining area or out on the back deck; the servers will find you when it's ready. Cash only; burgers run about $6.

Locals swear by **Rick's All Seasons Cafe** (240 York St., York, 207/363-5584), where the food is good, and the gossip is even better. Go for breakfast or lunch—the fried clams earn raves. Have patience: Almost everything is cooked to order. It's worth the wait.

Casual to Fine Dining

It's hard to know whether Food or Shopping is the right category for **Stonewall Kitchen** (Stonewall La., York, 207/351-2712 or 800/207-5267, www.stonewallkitchen.com), a phenomenally successful company that concocts imaginative condiments and other food products, many of which have received national awards. The headquarters building—including a handsome shop with tasting areas and a "viewing gallery" where you can watch it all happen—is next to the Yorks Chamber of

Commerce building, on Route 1. Go hungry: There are an espresso bar and an excellent café on the premises, open daily for breakfast and lunch and light fare in the late afternoon. Dinner may be served during peak season; call.

Don't let the forlorn and faded exterior deter you. Serving "food that loves you back," **Frankie and Johnny's Natural Foods** (1594 Rte. 1 N, Cape Neddick, 207/363-1909, www.frankie-johnnys.com, opens 5 P.M. Wed.–Sun., $17–26) is vibrant inside. Chef/owner John Shaw's eclectic menu varies from bean-curd satay, vegan delight, and Cajun crab cakes to toasted peppercorn-seared sushi-grade tuna, blackened pork Delmonico, and smoked mozzarella ravioli. It's the best vegetarian menu in York, and the house-made pastas are excellent. Reservations are recommended for summer weekends. Be forewarned: Portions are more than generous. No credit cards ("plastic is not natural"). BYOB.

For a memorable meal, book a table at ◖ **Chapman Cottage** (370 York St., P.O. Box 575, York Harbor 03911, 207/363-2059 or 877/363-2059, www.chapmancottage-bandb.com). Dinner is served in two connected rooms, each with fireplace, and both are decorated in a style fitting the 1899 home. Nicely spaced tables, soft lighting, classical music, and comfortable chairs make it easy to settle in for a night of leisurely fine dining. Service is professional without being stuffy, and the menu is small but intriguing, with selections such as stuffed pork tenderloin, hazelnut ravioli, and duck ($18–27).

The glass-walled dining room at the **York Harbor Inn** (5:30–9:30 P.M. daily and 9:30 A.M.–2:30 P.M. Sun. brunch) gets high marks for creative cuisine (the head chef has been here since 1982), so reservations are essential. Entrées run $25–35. Ask about an early-bird special.

Renowned Boston chef Lydia Shire's new restaurant **Blue Sky on York Beach** (Rte. 1A, York Beach, 207/363-0050) is adding a new tone to downtown York Beach. Opened in late 2007, the second-floor restaurant in The Atlantic House is elegant yet welcoming, with gleaming wood floors, a see-through fireplace, white chairs, and big windows taking in the views. In summer, dinner also will be served on the ocean-view porch. The dining room opens nightly at 5:30 P.M. The menu ranges from pizza to lobster, with most entrées around $20; a lounge menu is less pricey. For more casual eats, try Shire's first-floor cafe, **Clara's Cupcake Café,** named after her granddaughter and serving sandwiches, soups, and baked goods.

Lobster

Before heading for the **Cape Neddick Lobster Pound/Harborside Restaurant** (Shore Rd., Cape Neddick, 207/363-5471), check the tide calendar. The rustic shingled building dripping with lobster-pot buoys has a spectacular harbor view (especially from the deck) at high tide, a rather drab one at low tide, so plan accordingly. Entrées are $15–24. Open at noon daily. It offers entertainment beginning at 10 P.M. Friday and Saturday in summer.

INFORMATION AND SERVICES

The Maine Tourism Association operates a Maine State Visitor Information Center (207/439-1319) in Kittery, between Route 1 and I-95, with access from either road. It's chock-full of brochures and has restrooms and a picnic area.

For York area information, head for the Shingle-style palace of the Yorks Chamber of Commerce (1 Stonewall La., off Rte. 1, York, 207/363-4422, www.gatewaytomaine.org), at I-95's York exit. Inside are restrooms. It's open daily in summer.

GETTING AROUND

The Maine Turnpike, a toll road, is generally the fastest route, if you're trying to get between two towns. Route 1 parallels the turnpike, on the ocean side. It's mostly two lanes and is lined with shops, restaurants, motels, and other tourist-oriented sites, which means stop-and-go traffic that often slows to a crawl. If you're traveling locally, it's best to walk or use the local trolley systems, which have the bonus of saving you the agony of finding a parking spot.

The **York Trolley** (207/748-3030, www.york-trolley.com) provides a number of options for getting around the Yorks. A York tour departs hourly 10 A.M.–2 P.M. Monday and Friday with stops at Short Sands, York Village, York Harbor, York Beach, and Nubble Lighthouse. A day pass is $8 adult, $4 kids 3–10.

The company also operates a **York Beach Shuttle** from late June to early September. The service between Long and Short Sands beaches runs every 30 minutes 9:30 A.M.–10:30 P.M. ($1.50 one-way, $3 complete loop).

The **Shoreline Shuttle** operates hourly between York's Short Sands Beach and Ogunquit's Perkins Cove from late June through Labor Day. Fare is $1 each way; a 12-ride pass is $10; 18 and younger ride free.

Ogunquit and Wells

Ogunquit has been a holiday destination since the indigenous residents named it "beautiful place by the sea." What's the appeal? An unparalleled, unspoiled beach, several top-flight (albeit pricey) restaurants, a dozen art galleries, and a respected art museum with a view second to none. The town has been home to an art colony attracting the glitterati of the painting world starting with Charles Woodbury in the late 1880s. The summertime crowds continue, multiplying the minuscule year-round population of just under 1,400. These days, it's an especially gay-friendly community, too. Besides the beach, the most powerful magnet is Perkins Cove, a working fishing enclave that looks more like a movie set. The best way to approach the cove is via trolley-bus or on foot, along the shoreline Marginal Way from downtown Ogunquit—midsummer parking in the cove ($3 per hour) is madness.

Wells, once the parent of Ogunquit and since 1980 its immediate neighbor to the north, was settled in 1640. Nowadays, it's best known as a long, skinny, family-oriented community with about 10,300 year-round residents, seven miles of splendid beachfront, and heavy-duty commercial activity: lots of antiques and used-book shops, and a handful of factory outlets. It also claims two spectacular nature preserves worth a drive from anywhere. At the southern end of Wells, abutting Ogunquit, is **Moody,** an enclave named after 18th-century settler Samuel Moody and even rating its own post office.

If swimming isn't your top priority, plan to visit Ogunquit and Wells after Labor Day, when crowds let up, lodging rates drop dramatically, weather is still good, and you can find restaurant seats and parking spots.

SIGHTS
◖ Ogunquit Museum of American Art (OMAA)

Not many museums can boast a view as stunning as the one at the Ogunquit Museum of American Art (543 Shore Rd., P.O. Box 815, Ogunquit 03907, 207/646-4909, www.ogunquitmuseum.org), nor can many communities boast such renown as a summer art colony. Overlooking Narrow Cove, 1.4 miles south of downtown Ogunquit, the museum prides itself on its distinguished permanent collection. Works of Marsden Hartley, Rockwell Kent, Walt Kuhn, Henry Strater, and Thomas Hart Benton, among others, are displayed in five galleries. Special exhibits are mounted each summer, when there is an extensive series of lectures, concerts, and other programs. OMAA has a well-stocked gift shop, wheelchair access, and landscaped grounds with sculptures, a pond, and manicured lawns. Admission is $7 adults, $5 seniors, $4 students, and free for kids under 12. It's open 10:30 A.M.–5 P.M. Mon.–Sat., 2–5 P.M. Sunday July 1 to late October; closed Labor Day and for four days in mid-August for rehanging.

◖ Marginal Way

No visit to Ogunquit is complete without a leisurely stroll along the Marginal Way, the mile-long foot path edging the ocean from Shore Road (by the Sparhawk Resort) to Perkins Cove. It's been a must-walk since Josiah

© TOM NANGLE

The Marginal Way was a gift to the town of Ogunquit in the 1920s.

Chase gave the right-of-way to the town in the 1920s. The best times to appreciate this shrub-lined, shorefront walkway in Ogunquit are early morning or when everyone's at the beach. En route are tide pools, intriguing rock formations, crashing surf, pocket beaches, benches (though the walking's a cinch, even partially wheelchair-accessible), and a marker listing the day's high and low tides. When the surf's up, keep a close eye on the kids—the sea has no mercy. A midpoint access is at Israel's Head (behind a sewage plant masquerading as a tiny lighthouse), but getting a parking space is pure luck. Best advice is to stroll the Marginal Way to Perkins Cove for lunch, shopping, and maybe a boat trip, and then return to downtown Ogunquit via trolley-bus.

Perkins Cove

Turn-of-the-20th-century photos show Ogunquit's Perkins Cove lined with gray-shingled shacks used by a hardy colony of local fishermen—fellows who headed offshore to make a tough living in little boats. They'd hardly recognize it today. Though the cove remains a working lobster-fishing harbor, several old shacks have been reincarnated as boutiques and restaurants, and photographers go crazy shooting the quaint inlet spanned by a little pedestrian drawbridge. In midsummer, you'll waste precious time looking for one of the three or four dozen parking places ($3 an hour), so take advantage of the trolley-bus service. In the cove are galleries, gift shops, a range of eateries (fast food to lobster to high-end dining—see *Ogunquit* under *Food*), boat excursions, and public restrooms.

◖ Wells Reserve at Laudholm Farm

Known locally as Laudholm Farm (the name of the restored 19th-century visitors center), Wells National Estuarine Research Reserve (342 Laudholm Farm Rd., Wells, 207/646-1555, www.wellsreserve.org) occupies 1,690 acres of woods, beach, and coastal salt marsh on the southern boundary of the Rachel Carson National Wildlife Refuge, just

Laudholm Farm is the site of the Wells National Estuarine Research Reserve.

one-half mile east of Route 1. Seven miles of trails wind through the property. The best trail is the Salt Marsh Loop, with a boardwalk section leading to an overlook with panoramic views of the marsh and Little River inlet. Another winner is the Barrier Beach Walk, 1.3-mile round-trip that goes through multiple habitats all the way to beautiful Laudholm Beach. Allow 1.5 hours for either; you can combine the two. Lyme disease ticks have been found here, so tuck pant legs into socks and stick to the trails (some of which are wheelchair-accessible). The informative exhibits in the visitors center (open 10 A.M. to 4 P.M. Mon.–Sat. and noon–4 P.M. Sun. May–Oct., weekdays Oct.–Mar., closed mid-Dec.–mid-Jan.) make a valuable prelude for enjoying the reserve. An extensive program schedule, April–November, includes lectures, nature walks, and children's programs. Reservations are required for some programs. Trails are accessible 7 A.M.–dusk. From late May to mid-October, admission is charged, $2 adult, $1 ages 6–16.

Rachel Carson National Wildlife Refuge

Ten chunks of coastal Maine real estate—now more than 4,700 acres, eventually 7,600 acres, between Kittery Point and Cape Elizabeth—make up this refuge (Rte. 9, 321 Port Rd., Wells, 207/646-9226, http://rachelcarson.fws.gov) headquartered at the northern edge of Wells, near the Kennebunkport town line. Pick up a *Carson Trail Guide* at the refuge office (parking space is very limited) and follow the mile-long walkway (wheelchair-accessible) past tidal creeks, salt pans, and salt marshes. It's a birder's paradise during migration seasons. As with the Laudholm Farm reserve, the Lyme disease tick has been found here, so tuck pant legs into socks and stick to the trail. Office hours are 8 A.M.–4:30 P.M. weekdays year-round; trail access is sunrise to sunset, year-round. Leashed pets are allowed.

Ogunquit Arts Collaborative Gallery

Closer to downtown Ogunquit is the

Ogunquit Arts Collaborative Gallery (also known as the Barn Gallery, Shore Rd. and Bourne La., P.O. Box 529, Ogunquit 03907, 207/646-8400), featuring the works of member artists—an impressive group. The OAC is the showcase for the Ogunquit Art Association, established by Charles Woodbury, who was inspired to open an art school in Perkins Cove in the late 19th century. Special programs throughout the season include concerts, workshops, gallery talks, and an art auction. The gallery is open 11 A.M.–5 P.M. Monday–Saturday and 1–5 P.M. Sunday late May–Oct. 1. Admission is free.

Wells Auto Museum

More than 80 vintage vehicles, plus a collection of old-fashioned nickelodeons (bring nickels and dimes, they work), are jam-packed into the Wells Auto Museum (Rte. 1, Wells, 207/646-9064). From the outside, it just looks like a big warehouse, right on the highway. Admission is $5 adults, $2 children 6–12. It's open 10 A.M.–5 P.M. daily Memorial Day–Columbus Day.

Local History Museums

Ogunquit's history is preserved in the **Ogunquit Heritage Museum** (86 Obeds La., Dorothea Jacobs Grant Common, Ogunquit, 207/646-0296, www.ogunquitheritagemuseum.org, 12:30–4:30 P.M. Tues.–Sat. June–Sept.). The museum opened in 2002 in the restored Captain James Winn House, a 1785 cape listed on the National Register. Plans call for the construction of a fishing shack and boat shop to display appropriate exhibits, including an Ogunquit dory.

Right on the historic Post Road that once linked Boston with points north stands the **Historic Meetinghouse Museum** (938 Post Rd., Rte. 1, opposite Wells Plaza, P.O. Box 801, Wells 04090, 207/646-4775, 10 A.M.–4 P.M. Tues.–Thurs., to 1 P.M. Sat. June–mid. Oct, Wed. and Thurs. only in winter), a handsome steepled structure on the site of the town's first church (1643). Preserved and maintained by the Historical Society of Wells and Ogunquit,

its displays include old photos, ship models, needlecraft, and local memorabilia. On the second floor is a genealogical library where volunteers will help you research your roots. Enter in the rear.

RECREATION
Beaches

One of Maine's most scenic and unspoiled sandy beachfronts, the 3.5-mile stretch of sand fringed with seagrass is a major magnet for hordes of sunbathers, spectators, swimmers, surfers, and sandcastle builders. Getting there means crossing the Ogunquit River via one of three access points. For Ogunquit's **Main Beach**—with a spanking new bathhouse and high crowd content—take Beach Street. To reach **Footbridge Beach,** marginally less crowded, either take Ocean Street and the footbridge or take Bourne Avenue to Ocean Avenue in adjacent Wells and walk back toward Ogunquit. **Moody Beach,** at Wells's southern end, technically is private property—a subject of considerable legal dispute. Lifeguards are on duty all summer at the public beaches, and there are restrooms in all three areas. The beach is free, but parking is not; parking lots charge by the hour ($4 an hour at the Main Beach) or the day ($15 per day at Main Beach, Footbridge Beach, and Moody Beach), and they fill up early on warm midsummer days. After 3 P.M., some are free. It's far more sensible to opt for the frequent trolley-buses.

Wells beaches continue where Ogunquit's leave off. **Crescent Beach,** Webhannet Drive between Eldredge and Mile Roads, is the tiniest, with tide pools, no facilities, and limited parking. **Wells Beach,** Mile Road to Atlantic Avenue, is the major (and most crowded) beach, with lifeguards, restrooms, and parking. Around the other side of Wells Harbor is **Drakes Island Beach** (take Drakes Island Road, at the blinking light), a less crowded spot with restrooms and lifeguards. Walk northeast from Drakes Island Beach and you'll eventually reach Laudholm Beach, with great birding along the way. Summer beach-parking permits are available from the town hall in Wells: it's $15 a day for nonresidents ($5 for a motorcycle,

$25 for an RV); if you're staying longer, a $50 10-visit pass is a better bargain.

Bike, Kayak, and Surfboard Rentals

At **Wheels and Waves** (579 Post Rd., Rte. 1, Wells, 207/646-5774, www.wheelsnwaves.com), mountain-bike rentals begin at $20 a day; tandems are $40. Surfboards are $25.

Put in right at the harbor and explore the estuary from **Webhannet River Kayak and Canoe Rentals** (345 Harbor Rd., Wells, 207/646-9649, www.webhannetriver.com). Rates begin at $25 for two hours.

Boating Excursions

Depending on your interest, you can go deep-sea fishing or whale-watching or just gawking out of Perkins Cove, Ogunquit. Between April and early November, Captain Tim Tower runs half-day (departing 4 P.M.; $45 pp) and full-day (departing 7 A.M.; $70 pp) **deep-sea-fishing trips** aboard the 40-foot *Bunny Clark* (P.O. Box 837, Ogunquit 03907, 207/646-2214, www.bunny-clark.com). Reservations are necessary. Tim has a science degree, so he's a wealth of marine biology information. All gear is provided, and the crew'll fillet your catch for you; dress warmly and wear sunblock.

Perkins Cove (Barnacle Billy's Dock) is also home port for the Hubbard family's **Finestkind Cruises** (207/646-5227, www.finestkind-cruises.com), offering 1.5-hour, 14-mile Nubble Lighthouse cruises (10 A.M., noon, 2 and 4 P.M. daily; $18 adults, $10 kids) and one-hour cocktail cruises (5:45 P.M. daily; two extra trips in July and Aug.; $12 adults, $7 kids; cash bar) in a sheltered powerboat. A 75-minute breakfast cruise, complete with coffee, juice, and muffin, departs at 9 A.M. daily ($15 adults, $10 kids). The family also does 50-minute lobster-boat trips, 4–6 cruises Monday–Saturday; look and listen—no helping; $12 adults, $7 kids) in a real lobster boat (no toilets). Also available are 1.75-hour sails aboard *The Cricket,* a locally built wooden sailboat. It departs three times daily and costs $27.50 pp. High season runs July 1 through Labor Day; limited schedule May, June, September, October. Reservations are

advisable but usually unnecessary midweek. No credit cards.

Golf

The 18-hole, Donald Ross–designed **Cape Neddick Country Club** (650 Shore Rd., 207/361-2011, www.capeneddickgolf.com) is a semiprivate 18-hole course with restaurant and driving range.

Sea Kayaking

World Within Sea Kayaking (746 Ocean Ave., Wells, 207/646-0455, www.worldwithin.com) has both tours and rentals. Rentals are available on the tidal Ogunquit River to experienced kayakers for $15/hour single, $25/hour double. Guided tours begin with one hour of land instruction followed by two hours on the water for $70 pp. World Within also has an outlet at Wheels and Waves.

ENTERTAINMENT

Theater

Having showcased top-notch professional theater since the 1930s, the 750-seat **Ogunquit Playhouse** (Rte. 1, P.O. Box 915, Ogunquit 03907, 207/646-5511, www.ogunquitplayhouse. org) knows how to do it right: presenting comedies and musicals each summer, with big-name stars. The air-conditioned building is wheelchair-accessible. The box office is open daily in season, beginning in early May. Performances are at 8 P.M. Tuesday–Friday, 8:30 P.M. Saturday, matinees at 2:30 P.M. Wednesday and Thursday and 3:30 P.M. Sunday mid-June–Labor Day. Prices range $39–48. The playhouse also presents a children's series and a handful of Sunday night concerts. Parking can be a hassle; consider walking the short distance from the Bourne Lane trolley-bus stop.

Live Music

Ogunquit has several nightspots with good reputations for food and live entertainment. Best known is **Jonathan's** (2 Bourne La., P.O. Box 1879, Ogunquit 03907, 207/646-4777 or 800/464-9934 in Maine), where national headliners often are on the schedule upstairs. Advance tickets are cheaper than at the door, and dinner guests get preference for seats. Reservations are essential at this popular spot. The well-respected downstairs restaurant has creative entrées for $18–30 and ethnic flavors at the oyster bar. Highlighting the dining room are contemporary artwork and a 600-gallon aquarium. It's open 5–9:30 P.M., to 10 P.M. Friday and Saturday.

Ogunquit Performing Arts (207/646-6170) presents a full slate of programs, including classical concerts, ballet, and theater.

The **Wells Summer Concert Series** runs from early July through early September at the Hope Hobbs Gazebo in Wells Harbor Park. A wide variety of music is represented, from sing-alongs to swing.

FESTIVALS AND EVENTS

The **Fourth of July** celebration on Ogunquit Beach includes fireworks and live music. **Harbor Fest,** a concert, craft fair, parade, chicken barbecue, and children's activities, takes place the second weekend of July in Harbor Park in Wells.

In mid-August, Ogunquit Beach hosts a **Sandcastle-Building Contest** and in late August is the annual **Sidewalk Art Show and Sale.**

Capriccio is a performing arts festival, with daytime and evening events as well as a kite festival, held during the first week of September. Then, the second weekend that month, Wells National Estuarine Research Reserve (Laudholm Farm) hosts the **Laudholm Nature Crafts Festival,** a two-day juried crafts fair with children's activities and guided nature walks. This is an especially fine event. And the *third* weekend of September, the **Annual Ogunquit Antiques Show** benefits the Historical Society of Wells and Ogunquit. It's held at the Dunaway Center, School Street, Ogunquit.

In late October is **OgunquitFest,** a family-oriented weeklong event with pumpkin decorating, scarecrow contest, and other seasonal activities.

Christmas by the Sea, the second weekend of December, features caroling, tree lighting,

shopping specials, Santa Claus, a chowderfest, and a beach bonfire in Ogunquit.

SHOPPING
Antiques and Antiquarian Books

Antiques are a Wells specialty. You'll find more than 50 shops, with a huge range of prices. The majority are on Route 1. **R. Jorgensen Antiques** (502 Post Rd., Rte. 1, R.R. 1, Box 1125, Wells 04090, 207/646-9444), is a phenomenon in itself, filling 11 showrooms in two buildings with European and American 18th- and 19th-century furniture and accessories. **MacDougall-Gionet Antiques and Associates** (2104 Post Rd., Rte. 1, Wells, 207/646-3531) has been here since the mid-1960s, and its reputation is stellar. The 65-dealer shop—in an 18th-century barn—carries American and European country and formal furniture and accessories.

If you've been scouring antiquarian bookshops for a long-wanted title, chances are you'll find it at **Douglas N. Harding Rare Books** (2152 Post Rd., Rte. 1, P.O. Box 184, Wells 04090, 207/646-8785 or 800/228-1398). Well cataloged and organized, the sprawling bookshop at any given time stocks upward of 100,000 books, prints, and maps, plus a hefty selection of Maine and New England histories. Don't count on leaving empty-handed—there are too many temptations.

Art Galleries

There's no scarcity of the spectacular scenery that drew artists to Ogunquit in the early 20th century, but it's not the artistic magnet it once was. Yet galleries have popped up here and there. After you've been to the art museum, do your art browsing along Shore Road and in Perkins Cove.

Lighthouse Extravaganza

Several minilighthouses stand watch over the **Lighthouse Depot** (Post Rd., Rte. 1, P.O. Box 1690, Wells 04090, 207/646-0608 or 800/758-1444, www.lighthousedepot.com), a truly amazing mecca for lighthouse aficionados. Imagine this: two floors of lighthouse books, sculptures, videos, banners, Christmas

© TOM NANGLE

The Cliff House Resort and Spa is on the edge of Bald Head.

ornaments, lawn ornaments, paintings, and replicas running the gamut from pure kitsch to attractive collectibles. Its *Maine Lighthouse Map and Guide* ($5.95) is particularly helpful for tracking down the state's sentinels. Depot owners Tim Harrison and Kathy Finnegan also publish the *Lighthouse Digest,* a monthly magazine focusing on North American lighthouses (annual subscription $28), and produce a large mail-order catalog. The shop is about 1.5 miles north of the junction of Routes 1 and 109.

ACCOMMODATIONS
Ogunquit

Motel-style accommodations are everywhere in Ogunquit, most along Route 1, yet finding last-minute rooms in July and August can be a challenge, so book well ahead if you'll be here then. Most properties are open only seasonally.

Hotels and Motels: You're almost literally within spitting distance of Perkins Cove at the 37-room **Riverside Motel** (159 Shore Rd., P.O. Box 2244, Ogunquit 03907, 207/646-2741, www.riversidemotel.com), where you can perch on your balcony and watch the action—or, for that matter, join it. Rooms with phone, air-conditioning, refrigerators, cable TV, and fabulous views are $130–160, with continental breakfast.

Juniper Hill Inn (336 Main St., Rte. 1, P.O. Box 2190, Ogunquit 03907, 207/646-4501 or 800/646-4544, www.ogunquit.com) is a particularly well-run motel-style lodging on five acres close to downtown Ogunquit and the beach. Amenities include refrigerators, cable TV, coin-operated laundry, fitness center, indoor and outdoor pools, and golf privileges. Rooms have all the amenities, plus free Wi-Fi. Peak rates are $149–219. Open all year.

You can't get much closer to the water than the **Above Tide Inn** (66 Beach St., P.O. Box 2188, Ogunquit 03907, 207/646-7454, www.abovetideinn.com, $170–250), which is built on a wharf over the tidal Ogunquit River and has views to the open Atlantic. It's steps from the beach and downtown Ogunquit. Each of the nine rooms has air-conditioning, TV, and minifridge; a light breakfast is provided; no in-room phone.

Cottage Colony: It's nearly impossible to land a peak-season cottage at **The Dunes** (518 Main St., P.O. Box 917, Ogunquit 03907, 207/646-2612, www.dunesonthewaterfront.com), but it's worth trying. The property is under its third generation of ownership and guests practically will their weeks to their descendents. Tidy, well-equipped white housekeeping cottages and a handful of guest rooms are generously spaced on a shady, grassy lawns that roll down to the river, with the dunes just beyond. Facilities include a dock with rowboats, pool, and lawn games. It's all meticulously maintained. In peak season, one- and two-bedroom cottages require a one- or two-week minimum stay; guest rooms require three nights. Rooms begin at $105, cottages at $190 per night; weekly cottage rentals begin at $1,330.

Eclectic Properties: It's not easy to describe the **Sparhawk Oceanfront Resort** (41 Shore Rd., P.O. Box 936, Ogunquit 03907, 207/646-5562), a sprawling, one-of-a-kind place popular with honeymooners, sedate families, and seniors. There's lots of tradition in this thriving, six-acre complex—it's had various incarnations since the turn of the 20th century—and the Happily Filled sign regularly hangs out front. Out back is the Atlantic, with forever views, and the Marginal Way starts right here. It offers tennis courts, gardens, heated freshwater pool. No restaurant, but Ogunquit has plenty of options, and breakfast is included with your room. The 87 rooms vary in the different buildings—from motel-type rooms (best views) and suites to inn-type suites; rates run $170–300 (seven-night minimum July 4 to mid-August).

Nor is it easy to describe **The Beachmere Inn** (62 Beachmere Pl., Ogunquit, 207/646-2021 or 800/336-3983, www.beachmere inn.com, $150–390), a private, oceanfront property comprising a Victorian-style inn, an updated motel, and other buildings as well as its own beaches. All rooms have air-conditioning, TV, and phone; many rooms have kitchenettes; most have balconies, decks, or terraces; some have fireplaces. Morning coffee and muffins are provided. Reservations require three-night to one-week minimum in July and August; closed January–late March.

Bed-and-Breakfasts: Built in 1899 for a prominent Maine lumbering family, 【 **Rockmere Lodge** (40 Stearns Rd., P.O. Box 278, Ogunquit 03907, 207/646-2985, www .rockmere.com, $160–225 peak), underwent a meticulous six-month restoration in the early 1990s, thanks to preservationists Andy Antoniuk and Bob Brown, and in 2006 the duo, along with Doug Flint, gave the inn and grounds a complete rejuvenation, lightening the decor. Near the Marginal Way on a peaceful street, the handsome home has eight very comfortable Victorian guest rooms, all with CD players and cable TV (a 1,000-title library of DVDs and VCR tapes and CDs is available) and most with ocean views. Rates include a generous breakfast, with a hot entrée every other day. A wraparound veranda, a gazebo, and "The Lookout," a third-floor windowed nook with comfy chairs, make it easy to settle in and just watch the passersby on the Marginal Way. The woodwork throughout is gorgeous, and the grounds double as a public garden. Beach towels, chairs, and umbrellas are provided for guests. Closed March and April. No pets; four dogs in residence.

Floors glisten, brass gleams, and breakfast is served on the glass-walled porch at the **Hartwell House** (118 Shore Rd., P.O. Box 393, Ogunquit 03907, 207/646-7210 or 800/235-8883, www.hartwellhouseinn.com, $175–300), where the 13 rooms and three good-sized suites, all with air-conditioning, are divided between two buildings straddling Shore Road. Rooms are beautifully decorated with antiques and reproductions; try for a garden-view room in the main house. Rates include a full breakfast and afternoon tea.

Resorts: Founded in 1872, **The Cliff House Resort and Spa** (Shore Rd., P.O. Box 2274, Ogunquit 03907, 207/361-1000), a self-contained Victorian-era complex, sprawls over 70 acres topping the edge of Bald Head Cliff, midway between the centers of York and Ogunquit. Third-generation innkeeper Kathryn Weare keeps updating and modernizing the facilities. Among the most recent additions are a spa building with oversize rooms with king-size beds, gas fireplaces, and balconies, as well as a full-service spa, indoor pool, outdoor vanishing-edge pool, and glass-walled fitness center overlooking the Atlantic. A new central check-in building with indoor amphitheater connects the main building to the spa building. The 150 room and suite styles and prices vary widely in decor, from old-fashioned to contemporary; all have cable TV and phones, some have gas fireplaces, most have a spectacular ocean view ($265–370). Packages are the way to go here. Other facilities include a dining room, lounge, family indoor and outdoor pools, games room, and tennis courts. Eight pet-friendly rooms ($25 per night) have bowl, bed, and treats, and there's a fenced-in exercise area. Open late March– early December.

Wells

Like Ogunquit, Wells has a long list of motel-type lodgings, mostly on Route 1, and everything fills up in late July and early August. If you're arriving then, don't count on finding last-minute space.

Once part of a giant 19th-century dairy farm, the **Beach Farm Inn** (97 Eldredge Rd., Wells, 207/646-8493, www.beachfarm inn.com) is a 2.5-acre oasis in a rather congested area 0.2 mile off Route 1. Guests can swim in the pool, relax in the library, or walk one-quarter mile down the road to the beach. If you bring your own bikes, storage is provided; rentals are available within walking distance. Eight rooms (five with private baths, two detached) are $100–135 d, including a full breakfast; two cottages go for $650 and $950 a week. Third-floor rooms have air-conditioning. Open all year.

Even closer to the beach is ◖ **Haven by the Sea** (59 Church St., Wells Beach, 207/646-4194, www.havenbythesea.com, $169–350), a lovely and modern B&B in a former church. Innkeepers John and Susan Jarvis have kept the original floor plan, which allows some surprises. Inside are hardwood floors, cathedral ceilings, and stained-glass windows. The confessional is now a full bar, and the altar has been converted to a dining area that opens to a marsh-view terrace—the bird-watching is superb. Guest rooms have sitting areas, and the suite has a whirlpool tub and fireplace. Guests have plenty of room to relax, including a living area with fireplace. Rates include a full breakfast and afternoon hors d'oeuvres. Also available are a three-bedroom, ocean-view cottage and an apartment.

FOOD
Ogunquit

Local Flavors: The Egg and I (501 Maine St., Rte. 1, 207/646-8777, www.eggandibreakfast.com) earns high marks for its omelettes and waffles. You can't miss it—there's always a crowd. Open 6 A.M.–2 P.M. daily for breakfast, with lunch choices also served after 11 A.M. No credit cards.

Equally popular is **Amore Breakfast** (178 Shore Rd., 207/646-6661, www.amore breakfast.com, 7 A.M.–1 P.M. Fri.–Tues.). Choose from a baker's dozen omelettes, seven versions of eggs Benedict (including lobster and a spirited rancheros version topped with salsa and served with guacamole), as well as various French toast, waffles, and all the regulars and irregulars.

Eat in or take out from **Village Food Market** (Main St., Ogunquit Center, 207/646-2122, www.villagefoodmarket.com). A breakfast sandwich is less than $3; subs and sandwiches are available in three sizes, and there's even a children's menu.

Scrumptious baked goods, tantalizing salads, and panini sandwiches are available to go at Mary Breen's fabulous ◖ **Bread and Roses** (28A Main St., 207/646-4227, www.breadandrosesbakery.com), a small bakery right downtown with a few tables outside.

Harbor Candy Shop (26 Main St.,

207/646-8078 or 800/331-5856) is packed with the most outrageous chocolate imaginable. Fudge, truffles, and turtles are all made here in the shop. Fortunately (or maybe unfortunately), it also accepts mail orders. Open all year.

Lobster: Creative marketing, a knockout view, and efficient service help explain why more than 1,000 pounds of lobster bite the dust every summer day at **Barnacle Billy's** (Perkins Cove, 207/646-5575 or 800/866-5575, 11 A.M.–9 P.M. daily seasonally). For ambience, stick with the original operation; Barnacle Billy's Etc., next door (formerly the Whistling Oyster), is an upmarket version of the same thing with a broader menu. Full liquor license. Try for the deck, with a front-row seat on Perkins Cove.

Ethnic: The closest thing to an upscale-rustic French country inn is the dining room at **◖ Provence,** also referred to as 98 Provence (262 Shore Rd., 207/646-9898, www.98provence.com). Chef/owner Pierre Gignac produces the cuisine to match, turning out appetizers such as stewed pheasant in baked tomato and chevre gratin and superb entrées in the $26–33 range, but there are also three fixed menus (around $29–37). Duck, venison, seafood, veal, and lamb are all represented. Service is attentive and well paced. Don't miss it, and be sure to make reservations. Open for the season at 5:30 P.M. Wednesday–Monday beginning in mid-April.

Cross the street from Provence and you're in Italy—sort of. Vegetarians and pasta fanatics gravitate to **The Impastable Dream** (261 Shore Rd., 207/646-3011, www.impastabledream.com). Entrée range is $12–19; choices are predictable (ravioli, gnocchi, lasagna, Mediterranean tomato-based sauces over pasta, etc.) in this comfortable, casual spot. No reservations, so you may have to wait. It's open 5–9 P.M. daily, and a kids' menu is available until 6 P.M.

The best and most authentic Italian dining is at **Angelina's Ristorante** (655 Main St./ Rte. 1, 207/646-0445), opened by popular local chef and owner David Giarusso in late 2005. Dine in the dining room or lounge or out on the deck, choosing from pastas, risottos (the house specialty), and main courses such as *rollantini di pollo,* a boneless chicken breast stuffed with prosciutto, mozzarella, and basil and baked with a light spinach cream sauce, or a hand-cut filet mignon grilled and finished with a chianti-portobello-gorgonzola demi-glace. More than 30 wines are available by the glass. Most choices run $16–24. It opens nightly at 5 P.M.

Casual Dining: Gypsy Sweethearts (10 Shore Rd., 207/646-7021, www.gypsysweethearts.com, 5:30–9 P.M. Tues.–Sun.) serves in four rooms on the ground floor of a restored house, and on a rooftop deck, too. It's one of the region's most reliable restaurants, and the creative menu is infused with ethnic accents and includes vegetarian choices (entrées $17–30). Seating is both inside and out. Reservations advised in midsummer.

Equally reliable, and just south of it is **Five-O** (50 Shore Rd., 207/646-6365, www.five-oshoreroad.com, 5–10 P.M. daily), where executive chef Jonathan MacAlpine turns out classics with flair complemented by well-conceived inspirations. The menus changes frequently, but entrées such as pan-seared Atlantic salmon or Peking chicken are $25–33. Lighter fare ($9–16) is available in the lounge to 11 P.M., where martinis are a specialty. Service is excellent. In the off-season, multicourse regional dinners are held about once a month ($70). There's even valet parking.

The View's the Thing: There's not much between you and Spain when you get a window seat at **MC** (Oarweed La., Perkins Cove, Ogunquit, 207/646-6263, www.mcperkinscove.com), sister restaurant of the mega-high-end Arrows Restaurant. Actually, almost every table on both floors has a view, and the sophisticated decor doesn't compete with it. Service is extremely attentive, and the food is fab, creative, and in keeping with chefs Mark Gaier and Clark Frasier, ultrafresh. If you can't justify the splurge for Arrows, get a taste of their cuisine here. Reservations are essential for dinner. It's open 11:30 A.M.–2:30 P.M. for lunch (entrées $9–19) and 5:30–11 P.M. for dinner (entrées $22–34), with a bar menu served until 11 P.M. A jazz brunch is served beginning at 11 A.M. Sundays. Closed Tuesdays and January.

Equally if not more impressive are the views from the dining room at **The Cliff House** (Shore Rd., Ogunquit, 207/361-1000), open to the public for breakfast, lunch, and dinner daily. Try for the brunch buffet, 7:30 A.M.–1 P.M. Sunday. Service can be so-so. Reservations are required for dinner (no jeans, T-shirts, or sneakers); entrée range is $23–33. Before or after dining, wander the grounds. Open late March–early December.

Destination Dining: Restrain yourself for a couple of days and then splurge on an elegant dinner at **Arrows** (Berwick Rd., about 1.5 miles west of Rte. 1, Ogunquit, 207/361-1100, www.arrowsrestaurant.com), definitely one of Maine's finest restaurants. In a beautifully restored 18th-century farmhouse overlooking well-tended gardens (including a one-acre kitchen garden that supplies about 90 percent of the produce), co-owners/chefs Mark Gaier and Clark Frasier do everything right here, starting with the artistic presentation. Prices are stratospheric by Maine standards—with wine and all, count on paying at least $250 a couple—but well worth it. "Innovative" is too tame to describe the menu; entrées cost close to $50. Consider the six-course tasting menu ($95); serious foodies might splurge on the indulgence tasting menu, 10 courses for $135. A credit card is required for reservations—essential in midsummer and on weekends. Jackets are preferred for men; no shorts. It's open for dinner at 6 P.M. mid-April–early December: Tuesday–Sunday in July and August, Wednesday–Sunday in June and September–Columbus Day; mostly weekends other months. Off-season, ask about winemaker, regional, bistro nights, and specialty dinners and cooking classes (most $69–89 for a five-course meal).

Wells

Local Flavors: Best homemade doughnuts in Wells (and beyond), hands down, are at **Congdon's** Doughnuts** (Rte. 1, Wells, 207/646-4219). Also try the strata. Open 6 A.M.–3 P.M. daily for breakfast and lunch year-round, closed Tuesday.

Bean suppers are held 5–7 P.M. on the first Saturday of the month, May–October, at the Masonic Hall on Sanford Road, and on the second Saturday at the Wells Congregational Church, on Route 1.

Flo's (Rte. 1, Wells, 11 A.M.–7 P.M. daily), an offspring of the York institution, has opened a stand in Wells. The famous hot dogs are served, but so are burgers and sandwiches. Order at the window, and then grab a picnic table under the pines.

For scrumptious baked goods and made-to-order sandwiches, head to **Borealis Bread** (Rte. 1, Wells, 8:30 A.M.–5:30 P.M. Mon.–Fri., 9 A.M.–4 P.M. Sat. and Sun.), in the Aubuchon Hardware plaza adjacent to the Wells Auto Museum. There are only two tables inside, so take it to the beach.

Pick up all sorts of fresh goodies at the **Wells Farmers Market** in the Town Hall parking lot, 3–6 P.M. Wednesdays.

Family Favorites: No eatery in this category qualifies as heart healthy, so don't say you weren't forewarned.

Longtime favorite **Billy's Chowder House** (216 Mile Rd., just off Rte. 1, 207/646-7558, www.billyschowderhouse.com) has a prime marsh-view location—with wall-to-wall cars in the parking lot. Seafood is the specialty here, but you can get just about anything. It's open 11:30 A.M.–10 P.M. July and August, to 9 P.M. other months, mid-January–early December.

The **Maine Diner** (2265 Post Rd., Rte. 1, Wells, 207/646-4441, www.mainediner.com) has a reputation built on lobster pie and award-winning seafood chowder. Beer and wine only. It's open 7 A.M.–9:30 P.M. (8 P.M. in winter) daily for breakfast, lunch, and dinner (breakfast available anytime). Prices run from less than $10 for diner food to $20 for surf and turf.

Newest among the family favorites is **Mainiax Restaurant** (Rte. 1, Wells, 207/646-0808, www.mainiaxrestaurant.com, 11:30 A.M.–8 P.M., to 9 P.M. Fri. and Sat.) The menu is huge—everyone in the family is sure to find something, the prices are moderate, and the decor is moosey. It's casual and fun.

Turf and Surf: A good steak in the land of lobster? You betcha. **The Steakhouse** (1205 Post Rd., Rte. 1, 207/646-4200, www.the-steakhouse.com, 4–9:30 P.M. Tues.–Sun.) is a great big barn of place where steaks are hand cut from USDA prime and choice, corn-fed Western beef that's never been frozen. Chicken, seafood, lobster (great stew), and even a vegetarian stir-fry are also on the menu (entrées $13–26); children's menu available. Service is efficient. No reservations, so be prepared for a wait. This place is *very* popular.

Locals rave about the seafood chowder and the lobster stew at **Lord's Harborside Restaurant** (Harbor Rd., Wells Harbor, 207/646-2651, www.lordsharborside.com, noon–9 P.M. Wed.–Mon., to 8 P.M. spring and fall). They should also rave about the view, a front-row seat on the Wells working harbor. Sure, it's touristy, but with these views, who cares? The menu has a bit of everything, but the emphasis is on fish and seafood, with most prices in the teens; lobster higher. Kids' menu available.

Fine Dining: Chef Joshua W. Mather has brought true fine dining to Wells with **Joshua's** (1637 Rte. 1, 207/646-3355, www.joshuas.biz). Chef Joshua grew up on his family's organic farm, just six miles distant, and produce from the farm highlights the menu. In a true family operation, his parents not only still work the farm, but they also work in the restaurant, a converted 1774 home with many of its original architectural elements. Everything is made on the premises, from the fabulous bread to the hand-churned ice cream. Entrées range $19–29. The Atlantic haddock, with carmelized onion crust, chive oil, and wild mushroom risotto is a signature dish and alone worth coming for. A vegetarian pasta entrée is offered nightly. Do save room for the maple walnut pie with maple ice cream. Yes, it's gilding the lily, but you can always walk the beach afterward. Reservations are essential for the dining rooms, but the full menu is also served in the bar. It's open 5–10 P.M. Monday–Saturday.

INFORMATION AND SERVICES

At the southern edge of Ogunquit, right next to the Ogunquit Playhouse, the Ogunquit Chamber of Commerce's Welcome Center (Rte. 1, Box 2289, Ogunquit 03907, 207/646-2939, www.ogunquit. org), provides all the usual visitor information, including restaurant menus. Ask for the *Touring and Trolley Route Map,* showing the Marginal Way, beach locations, and public restrooms. The chamber of commerce's annual visitor booklet thoughtfully carries a high-tide calendar for the summer. It also has public restrooms.

Just over the Ogunquit border in Wells (actually in Moody) is the Wells Information Center (Rte. 1 at Bourne Ave., P.O. Box 356, Wells 04090, 207/646-2451, www.wellschamber. org). A touch-pad kiosk takes over when the office is closed.

The handsome fieldstone Ogunquit Memorial Library (74 Shore Rd., Ogunquit, 207/646-9024) is the downtown's only National Historic Register building. Or visit the Wells Public Library (1434 Post Rd., Rte. 1, 207/646-8181, www.wells.lib. me.us).

GETTING THERE

Amtrak's **Downeaster** (800/872-7245, www .thedowneaster.com), which connects Boston's North Station with Portland, Maine, stops in Wells. The Shoreline Explorer trolley connects in season.

GETTING AROUND

The Maine Turnpike, a toll road, is generally the fastest route if you're trying to get between two towns. Route 1 parallels the turnpike, on the ocean side. It's mostly two lanes and is lined with shops, restaurants, motels, and other tourist-oriented sites, which means stop-and-go traffic that often slows to a crawl. If you're traveling locally, it's best to walk or use the local trolley systems, which have the bonus of saving you the agony of finding a parking spot.

Trolleys

The **Shoreline Explorer** (207/324-5762, www.shorelineexplorer.com) trolley system makes it possible to connect from York to Kennebunkport without your car. Each town's system is operated separately and has its own fees.

Ogunquit Trolley Co. (207/646-1411, www.ogunquittrolley.com) operates seasonal service in Ogunquit, with 39 stops (signposted) weaving through Ogunquit. Each time you board, it'll cost you $1.50 (kids 10 and younger $1), exact fare, but for the same price you can go the whole route—a great way to get your bearings—in about 40 minutes. Hours are 8:30 A.M.–8 P.M. late May–late June and Labor Day to Columbus Day, and 8 A.M.–11 P.M. late June–Labor Day.

Wells's seasonal **Shoreline Trolley System** on Route 1 runs every 20–30 minutes, 9 A.M.–11 P.M. late June–Labor Day. Fare is $1 per trip or $3 for a day pass; family day passes are also available. It operates between Wells and Kennebunk's Lower village.

Another option is the **Hotel Shuttle** (800/696-2463, www.shorelineexplorer.com), which operates between the Amtrak station in Wells and lodging properties within the Shoreline Explorer communities. Fares vary by zone and day, and reservation is required.

The Kennebunks

The world may have first learned of Kennebunkport when George Herbert Walker Bush was president, but Walkers and Bushes have owned their summer estate here for three generations. Visitors continue to come to the Kennebunks (the collective name for Kennebunk, Kennebunkport, Cape Porpoise, and Goose Rocks Beach—combined population about 15,200) hoping to catch a glimpse of the former first family, but they also come for the terrific ambience, the B&Bs, boutiques, boats, biking, and beaches.

The Kennebunks' earliest European settlers arrived in the mid-1600s. By the mid-1700s, shipbuilding had become big business in the area. Two ancient local cemeteries—North Street and Evergreen—provide glimpses of the area's heritage. Its Historic District reveals Kennebunk's moneyed past—the homes where wealthy shipowners and shipbuilders once lived, sending their vessels to the Caribbean and around the globe. Today, unusual shrubs and a dozen varieties of rare maples still line Summer Street—the legacy of ship captains in the global trade. Another legacy is the shiplap construction in many houses—throwbacks to a time when labor was cheap and lumber plentiful. Closer to the beach, in Lower Village, stood the workshops of sailmakers, carpenters, and mastmakers whose output drove the booming trade to success.

While Kennebunkport draws most of the sightseers and summer traffic, Kennebunk feels more like a year-round community. It boasts an interesting, old-fashioned downtown and a mix of shops, restaurants, and attractions. Yes, its beaches, too, are well known, but many visitors drive right through the middle of Kennebunk without stopping to enjoy its assets.

The Kennebunks are communities with conscience—loaded with conservationists working to preserve hikeable, bikeable green space for residents and visitors. Be sure not to miss these trails, bikeways, and offshore islets. Gravestone rubbers will want to check out Evergreen Cemetery, and history buffs should pick up a copy of *Walking in the Port,* the Kennebunkport Historical Society's well-researched booklet of three self-guided historic walking tours. To appreciate the area another way, climb aboard the Intown Trolley, with regular summertime service and lots of entertaining tidbits from the driver.

SIGHTS

◖ Seashore Trolley Museum

There's nothing quite like an antique electric trolley to dredge up nostalgia for bygone days. With a collection of more than 250

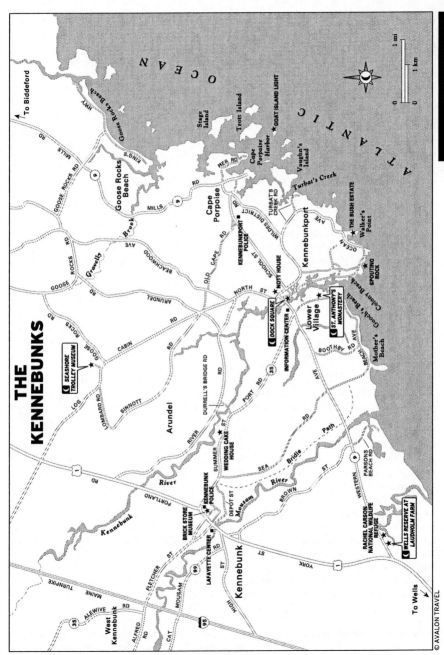

transit vehicles (more than two dozen trolleys on display), the Seashore Trolley Museum (195 Log Cabin Rd., P.O. Box A, Kennebunkport 04046, 207/967-2800, www.trolleymuseum.org) verges on trolley-mania. Whistles blowing and bells clanging, restored streetcars do frequent trips (between 10:05 A.M. and 4:15 P.M.) on a 3.5-mile loop through the nearby woods. Ride as often as you wish, then check out the activity in the streetcar workshop, and go wild in the trolley-oriented gift shop. Bring a picnic lunch and enjoy it here. Special events are held throughout the summer, including Ice Cream and Sunset Trolley Rides at 7 P.M. every Wednesday and Thursday in July and August. Cost is $4 and includes ice cream. And here's an interesting wrinkle: Make a reservation, plunk down $50, and you can have a one-hour "Motorman" experience driving your own trolley (with help, of course). Museum tickets are $8 adults, $6 seniors, $5.50 kids 6–16, and free for kids 5 and under. The museum is 1.7 miles southeast of Route 1. It's open 10 A.M.–5 P.M. daily mid-June–Columbus Day, and weekends in May, late October, and Christmas Prelude.

Walker's Point: The Bush Estate

There's no public access to Walker's Point, but you can join the sidewalk gawkers on Ocean Avenue overlooking George and Barbara Bush's summer compound. The 41st president and his wife lead a low-key, laid-back life when they're here, so if you don't spot them through binoculars, you may well run into them at a shop or restaurant in town. Intown Trolley's regular narrated tours go right past the house—or it's an easy, scenic family walk from Kennebunkport's Dock Square. On the way, you'll pass **St. Ann's Church,** whose stones came from the ocean floor, and the paths to **Spouting Rock** and **Blowing Cave**—two natural phenomena that create spectacular water fountains if you manage to be there midway between high and low tides.

Wedding Cake House

The Wedding Cake House (104 Summer St.,

Kennebunk) is a private residence, so you can't go inside, but it's one of Maine's most-photographed buildings. Driving down Summer Street (Rte. 35), midway between the downtowns of Kennebunk and Kennebunkport, it's hard to miss the yellow and white Federal mansion with gobs of gingerbread and Gothic Revival spires and arches. Built in 1826 by shipbuilder George Bourne as a wedding gift for his wife, the Kennebunk landmark remained in the family until 1983.

Cape Porpoise

When your mind's eye conjures an idyllic lobster-fishing village, it probably looks a lot like Cape Porpoise—only 2.5 miles from busy Dock Square. Follow Route 9 eastward from Kennebunkport; when Route 9 turns north, continue straight, and take Pier Road to its end. From the small parking area, you'll see lobster boats at anchor, a slew of working wharves, and 19th-century **Goat Island Light,** now automated, directly offshore. In Cape Porpoise are a handful of B&Bs, restaurants, galleries, historic Atlantic Hall, and the extra-friendly Bradbury Bros. Market.

Local History Museums

Occupying four restored 19th-century buildings (including the 1825 William Lord store) in downtown Kennebunk, **The Brick Store Museum** (117 Main St., Kennebunk, 207/985-4802, www.brickstoremuseum.org, 10 A.M.–4:30 P.M. Tues.–Fri. and 10 A.M.–1 P.M. Sat.) has garnered a reputation for unusual exhibits: a century of wedding dresses, a two-century history of volunteer firefighting, life in southern Maine during the Civil War. Admission is by donation ($5 suggested). The museum encourages appreciation for the surrounding Kennebunk Historic District with hour-long **architectural walking tours,** mid-June to mid-October (call for current schedule). Cost is $5. If the schedule doesn't suit, the museum sells a walk-it-yourself booklet for $5.

Owned and maintained by the Kennebunkport Historical Society, **The Nott House** (8

© TOM NANGLE

The Wedding Cake House was built by a local shipbuilder as a wedding gift for his wife.

Maine St., Kennebunkport) is a mid-19th-century Greek Revival mansion filled with Victorian furnishings. Be sure to visit the restored gardens. It's open 1–4 P.M. Tuesday–Friday and 10 A.M.–1 P.M. Saturday mid-June–Columbus Day. Tour tickets are $5 adults, under 18 are free. Hour-long architectural walking tours of the Kennebunkport Historic District depart from the Nott House at 11 A.M. Thursday and Saturday in July and August, and Saturday only in September. Cost is $3 pp. At the house, you can buy a guidebook for a do-it-yourself tour for $4.

The Kennebunkport Historical Society also owns and maintains a five-building **History Center** (125–135 North St., Kennebunkport, 207/967-2751, www.kporthistory.org). The Town House School, dating from the turn of the 20th century, is the society's research center. The Pasco Exhibit Center, containing the society's offices, also has permanent and rotating exhibits of local memorabilia. It's open 10 A.M.–4 P.M. Tuesday–Friday all year. Admission is $3 adults, free for children under

18. If you call ahead for an appointment, a staff member will let you into the tiny old jail on the grounds.

◖ Dock Square

Even if you're not a shopper, make it a point to meander through the heart of Kennebunkport's shopping district, where one-time fishing shacks have been restored and renovated into upscale shops, boutiques, galleries, and dining spots. Some shops, especially those on upper floors, offer fine harbor views. If you're willing to poke around a bit, you'll find some unusual items that make distinctive souvenirs or gifts—pottery, vintage clothing, books, specialty foods, and, yes, T-shirts.

PARKS AND PRESERVES

Thanks to a dedicated coterie of year-round and summer residents, the foresighted **Kennebunkport Conservation Trust (KCT),** founded in 1974, has become a nationwide model for land-trust organizations. The KCT has managed to preserve from development sev-

© HILARY NANGLE

Dock Square is the center of the action in busy Kennebunkport. Shops and restaurants make it easy to spend hours here browsing.

eral hundred acres of land (including 11 small islands off Cape Porpoise Harbor), and most of this acreage is accessible to the public, especially with a sea kayak. The trust has even assumed ownership of 7.7-acre Goat Island, with its distinctive lighthouse visible from Cape Porpoise and other coastal vantage points. Contact the KCT (P.O. Box 7028, Cape Porpoise 04014, www.thekennebunkportconservationtrust.org) for information on its holdings or to volunteer for trail maintenance.

◖ St. Anthony's Monastery

Long ago, 35,000 Native Americans used this part of town for a summer camp. They knew a good thing. So did a group of Lithuanian Franciscan monks who in 1947 fled war-ravaged Europe and acquired the 200-acre St. Anthony's Franciscan Monastery (Beach St., Kennebunk, mailing address P.O. Box 980, Kennebunkport 04046, 207/967-2011). From 1956 to 1969, they ran a high school here. The monks occupy the handsome Tudor great house, but the well-

tended grounds (sprinkled with shrines and a recently restored sculpture created by Vytautas Jonynas for the 1964 World's Fair) are open to the public sunrise–sunset. A short path leads from the monastery area to a peaceful gazebo overlooking the Kennebunk River. No pets or bikes. Public restrooms are available. The grounds are open 6 A.M.–8:30 P.M. in summer, closing at 6 P.M. in winter.

Vaughn's Island Preserve

Thanks to the Kennebunkport Conservation Trust, 96-acre Vaughn's Island has been saved for posterity. You'll need to do a little planning, tidewise, since the island is about 600 feet offshore. Consult a tide calendar and aim for low tide close to the new moon or full moon (when the most water drains away). Allow yourself an hour or so before and after low tide, but no longer, or you may need a boat rescue. Wear treaded rubber boots, since the crossing is muddy and slippery with rockweed. Keep an eye on your watch and explore the ocean (east) side of the island, along the beach. It's all worth the effort, and there's a great view of Goat Island Light off to the east. From downtown Kennebunkport, take Maine Street to Wildes District Road. Continue to Shore Road (also called Turbat's Creek Rd.), go 0.6 mile, jog left 0.2 mile more, and park in the tiny lot at the end.

Emmons Preserve

Also under the stewardship of the Kennebunkport Conservation Trust, the Emmons Preserve has two trails (blazed yellow and pink) meandering through 146 acres of woods and fields on the edge of Batson's River (also called Gravelly Brook). The yellow trail gives best access to the water. Fall colors here are brilliant, birdlife is abundant, and you can do a loop in half an hour. But why rush? This is a wonderful oasis in the heart of Kennebunkport. From Dock Square, take North Street to Beachwood Avenue (right turn) to Gravelly Brook Road (left turn). The trailhead is on the left.

Picnic Rock

About 1.5 miles up the Kennebunk River from the ocean, Picnic Rock is the centerpiece of the **Butler Preserve,** a 14-acre enclave managed by The Nature Conservancy. Well named, the rock is a great place for a picnic and a swim, but don't count on being alone. A short trail loops through the preserve. Consider bringing a canoe or kayak (or renting one) and paddle with the tide past beautiful homes and the Cape Arundel Golf Club. From Lower Village Kennebunk, take Route 35 west and hang a right onto Old Port Road. When the road gets close to the Kennebunk River, watch for a Nature Conservancy oak-leaf sign on the right. Parking is along Old Port Road; walk down through the preserve to Picnic Rock, right on the river.

RECREATION
Beaches

Ah, the beaches. The Kennebunks are well endowed with sand but not with parking spaces. Between mid-June and mid-September, you'll need to buy a **parking permit** ($10 a day,

$20 a week, $50 a season) from the Kennebunk Town Hall (4 Summer St., 207/985-3675) or the Kennebunkport Police Station (101 Main St., 207/967-4243) or the chamber of commerce. (The police station is open 24 hours; other locations are not.) *You need a separate pass for each town.* Many lodgings provide free permits for their guests—be sure to ask when making room reservations. Or you can avoid the parking nightmare altogether by hopping aboard the Intown Trolley, which goes right by the major beaches.

The main beaches in **Kennebunk** (east to west, stretching about two miles) are 3,346-foot-long Gooch's (most popular), Kennebunk (locally called Middle or Rocks Beach), and Mother's (a smallish beach next to Lords Point, where there's also a playground). Lifeguards are on duty at Gooch's and Mother's Beaches July–Labor Day. Mother's Beach is the home of the Kennebunk Beach Improvement Association. Ask locally about a couple of other beach options.

Kennebunkport's claim to beach fame is three-mile-long Goose Rocks Beach, one of the loveliest in the area. Parking spaces are scarce and biking on Route 9 can be dicey, so if sun and sand are your primary goals, the best solution is to book a room nearby. You'll be about five miles east of all the downtown action, however. To reach the beach, take Route 9 from Dock Square east and north to Dyke Road (Clock Farm Corner). Turn right and continue to the end (King's Hwy.).

The prize for tiniest beach goes to Colony (officially Arundel) Beach, near The Colony resort complex. It's close to many Kennebunkport lodgings and an easy walk from Dock Square.

Bicycling

A mandatory stop for anyone interested in bicycles and biking is **Cape-Able Bike Shop** (83 Arundel Rd., Town House Corners, Kennebunkport, 207/967-4382, www.capeablebikes.com), a local institution since 1974. The shop has all kinds of rentals and accessories, repairs your wounded gear, sponsors Saturday morning group rides, and provides a free area bike map and the best insider information. (The bike map is also available at the chamber of commerce.) One-day hybrid bike rental is $22. Road- or mountain-bike rental is $27 a day. Map, helmet, and lock are included. Delivery service is available, but the shop operates a seasonal outpost in Lower Village, next to the chamber of commerce.

Cape Abel also offers tours. The 10–15 mile Comfort Beach Tour lasts about 2.5–3 hours and costs $59 adults, $29 kids 15 and younger, including a snack. A Singletrack Adventure moderate to advanced mountain bike tour covers 6–8 miles and lasts about three hours and costs $59 adults, $29 kids, and includes a snack. Tours include rental bike, helmet, carry bag, and water bottle.

Golf

Three 18-hole golf courses make the sport a big deal in the area. **Cape Arundel Golf Club** (19 River Rd., Kennebunkport, 207/967-3494), established in 1897, and **Webhannet Golf Club** (8 Central Ave., Kennebunk, 207/967-2061), established in 1902, are semiprivate and open to nonmembers; call for tee times at least 24 hours ahead. At Cape Arundel, where George Bush plays, no jeans or sweatpants are allowed. In nearby Arundel, **Dutch Elm Golf Course** (5 Brimstone Rd., Arundel, 207/282-9850) is a public course with rentals, pro shop, and putting greens.

Whale Watches and Lobster-Boat Cruises

Whale sightings offshore include finbacks, minkes, and humpbacks, and the local cruise boats have had remarkable success. The 80-foot *Nick's Chance* (4 Western Ave., Lower Village, Kennebunk, 207/967-5507 or 800/767-2628, www.firstchancewhalewatch.com) departs twice daily in July and August for 4.5-hour whale watches to Jeffrey's Ledge, weather permitting. Cost is $40 adults, $25 children ages 3–12, $10 up to age 3. Departure is from Performance Marine in Kennebunk Lower Village (behind Bartley's Restaurant).

Under the same ownership and departing from the same location is the 65-foot open lobster boat *Kylie's Chance,* which departs four times daily in July and August for 1.5-hour scenic lobster cruses. A lobstering demonstration is given on most trips, but never on the evening one. Cost is $18 adults, $12 ages 3–12.

Boating Excursions

For day sailing, the 37-foot one-ton former racing yacht *Bellatrix* (95 Ocean Ave., Kennebunkport, 207/590-1125, www.sailing-trips.com) charges $50 pp for a three-hour sail. The handsome 55-foot gaff-rigged schooner *Eleanor* (Arundel Wharf, 43 Ocean Ave., Kennebunkport, 207/967-8809, www.gwi.net/schoonersails) heads out for two-hour sails, weather and tides willing, 1–3 times daily during the summer. Cost is $40 pp.

Canoe and Kayak Rentals

Explore the Kennebunk River. **Kennebunk-port Marina** (67 Ocean Ave., Kennebunkport, 207/967-3411) rents canoes and single kayaks for $25/two hours or $45 half day; double kayaks are $45/two hours or $60 half day. Hint: Check the tide before you depart, and plan your trip to paddle with it, rather than against it.

Sportfishing

Saltwater, light tackle, and fly sportfishing are the specialties of **Lady J Sportfishing Charters** (10 Kimball La., Kennebunk, 207/985-7304, www.ladyjcharters.com) aboard the *Rebecca Lynn.* Two-hour trips for kids ($175) include hauling lobster traps. Inshore trips for stripers and bluefish are $300 four hours, $400 six hours. Eight-hour specialty trips for shark or groundfish are $600. Trips leave from the Arundel Wharf Restaurant (Ocean Ave., Kennebunkport).

Surfing

If you want to catch a wave, stop by **Aquaholics Surf Shop** (166 Port Rd., Kennebunk, 207/967-8650, www.aquaholicsurf.com). The shop has boards, wetsuits, and related gear for

© TOM NANGLE

Boats are always coming and going in Kennebunkport's harbor.

both sale and rental, and it offers lessons and surf camps.

ENTERTAINMENT

Live entertainment is featured, mostly weekends, at Federal Jack's Brewpub and Windows on the Water, and at the Kennebunkport Inn and The Colony.

Kennebunk Parks and Recreation sponsors **Concerts in the Park,** a weekly series of free concerts 6:30–7:30 P.M. Wednesdays late June to mid-August, in Rotary Park on Water Street.

At 7 P.M. on Thursday evenings in July, the **River Tree Arts Summer Concert Series** brings music to the lawn of the South Congregational Church, Kennebunkport.

Live, professional summer theater is on tap at the **Arundel Barn Playhouse** (53 Old Post Rd., Arundel, 207/985-5552, www.arundelbarnplayhouse.com), with productions staged in a renovated 1888 barn, June–September; tickets $19–24.

River Tree Arts (RTA)

The area's cultural spearhead is River Tree Arts (35 Western Ave., Kennebunk, 207/967-9120, www.rivertreearts.org), an incredibly energetic, volunteer-driven organization that sponsors concerts, classes, workshops, exhibits, and educational programs throughout the year.

FESTIVALS AND EVENTS

Concerts and kids' activities are part of the **Summer Solstice Festival** in June. Take the kids to the **Kennebearport Teddy Bear Show,** usually the second Saturday in August, but watch the reactions of all the grown-ups.

The first two weekends of December mark the festive **Christmas Prelude,** during which spectacular decorations adorn historic homes, candle-toting carolers stroll through the Kennebunks, stores have special sales, and Santa Claus shows up in a lobster boat.

SHOPPING

Lots of small, attractive boutiques surround **Dock Square,** the hub of Kennebunkport, so gridlock often develops in midsummer. Avoid driving through here at the height of the season. Take your time and walk, bike, or ride the local trolley-bus.

Antiques and Art

English, European, and American furniture and architectural elements and garden accessories are just a sampling of what you'll find at **Antiques on Nine** (Rte. 9, Lower Village, Kennebunk, 207/967-0626). Another good place for browsing high-end antiques as well as home accents is **Hurlburt Designs** (Rte. 9, Lower Village, Kennebunk, 207/967-4110). More than 30 artists are represented at **Wright Gallery** (Pier Rd., Cape Porpoise, 207/967-5053).

Jean Briggs represents nearly 100 artists at her topflight **Mast Cove Galleries** (Maine St. and Mast Cove La., Kennebunkport, 207/967-3453), in a handsome Greek Revival house near the Graves Memorial Library. Prices vary widely, so don't be surprised if you spot something affordable. The gallery sponsors 2.5-hour Wednesday evening jazz concerts in July and August ($10 donation includes light refreshments). Call for the schedule. **The Gallery on Chase Hill** (10 Chase Hill Rd., Kennebunkport, 207/967-0049), in the stunningly restored Captain Chase House, next to the Windows on the Water restaurant, mounts rotating exhibits and represents a wide variety of Maine and New England artists. **Compliments** (Dock Sq., 207/967-2269) has a truly unique and fun collection of contemporary fine American crafts, with an emphasis on glass and ceramic wear.

Books, Clothing, and Gifts

The number of shops in this category in the Kennebunks is vast. You'll need to do your own exploring and discovering. Treasures are to be found all over the Kennebunks, but most are clustered around Dock Square (Kennebunkport) and in Lower Village (Kennebunk).

To appreciate the friendly, funky **Kennebunk Book Port** (10 Dock Sq., Kennebunkport, 207/967-3815 or 800/382-2710), climb to the second floor of the antique rum warehouse and read the shop slogan: "Ice cream, candy, children, bare feet, short, long, or no hair, cats, dogs, and small dragons are welcome anytime." This place has character.

Since 1968, **Port Canvas** (9 Ocean Ave., Kennebunkport, 207/985-9765 or 800/333-6788) has been turning out the best in durable cotton-canvas products. Need a new double-bottomed tote bag? It's here. Also here are golf-bag covers, belts, computer cases, day packs, and of course duffel bags.

Quilt fans should make time to visit **Mainely Quilts** (108 Summer St., Rte. 35, Kennebunk, 207/985-4250), behind the Waldo Emerson Inn. The shop has a nice selection of contemporary and antique quilts.

Most of the clothing shops clustered around Dock Square are rather pricey. Not so **Arbitrage** (28 Dock Sq., 207/967-9989), which combines designer consignment clothing with new fashions, vintage designer costume jewelry, shoes, and handbags.

Irresistible eye-dazzling costume jewelry, hair ornaments, handbags, lotions, cards, and other delightful finds fill every possible space at **Dannah** (123 Ocean Ave., Kennebunkport, 207/967-8640), in the Breakwater Spa building, with free customer-only parking in the rear.

Earth-Friendly Toiletries

Lafayette Center, a handsomely restored mill building housing boutiques and eateries, is also home to the **Tom's of Maine Natural Living Store** (Storer St., just off Main St., Kennebunk, 207/985-3874), an eco-sensitive local-turned-global firm that makes soaps, toothpaste, oils, and other products. "Factory seconds" are real bargains.

ACCOMMODATIONS

Rates listed are for peak season; most stay open through Christmas Prelude.

Inns and Hotels

Graciously dominating its 11-acre spread at the mouth of the Kennebunk River, **The Colony Hotel** (140 Ocean Ave. at King's Hwy., P.O. Box 511, Kennebunkport 04046,

207/967-3331 or 800/552-2363, www.thecolonyhotel.com/maine), springs right out of a bygone era, and its distinctive cupola is an area landmark. It's had a long-time commitment to the environment, with recycling, waste-reduction, and educational programs. There's a special feeling here, with cozy corners for reading, lawns and gardens for strolling, a beachfront swimming pool, room service, tennis privileges at the exclusive River Club, bike rentals, massage therapy, and lawn games. Doubles begin at $190, including breakfast, but not $5 pp daily service charge. Pets are $25 per night. Higher-priced rooms have ocean views, others have garden views. The hotel dining room is open to the public for breakfast, lunch, and dinner; reservations are advisable. Brunch is a big winner, 11 A.M.–2 P.M. Sunday mid-June–Labor Day. Open mid-May–late October.

The The White Barn Inn and its siblings have cornered the ultrahigh-end, boutique inn market, with four in this category. Most renowned is the **White Barn Inn** (37 Beach Ave., Kennebunk, mailing address P.O. Box 560, Kennebunkport 04046, 207/967-2321, www.whitebarninn.com, $340–780). Also part of the empire are **The Beach House Inn** (211 Beach Ave., Kennebunk, 207/967-3850, www.beachhseinn.com, $299–525), **The Breakwater Inn, Hotel, and Spa** (127 Ocean Ave., Kennebunkport, 207/967-3118, www.thebreakwaterinn.com, $290–345), **The Yachtsman Lodge and Marina** (Ocean Ave., Kennebunkport, 207/967-2511, www.yachtsmanlodge.com, $299–314), and three restaurants. Rooms in all properties have air-conditioning, phones, satellite TV, VCR and CD players; bikes and canoes are available for guests. Rates include bountiful continental breakfasts and afternoon tea, but check out the off-season packages, especially if you wish to dine at one of the restaurants. All but the Beach House are within easy walking distance of Dock Square.

The White Barn Inn is the most exclusive, with five-diamond and Relais and Chateaux status. It's home to one of the best restaurants in the *country*. Many rooms have fireplaces

and marble baths with separate steam showers and whirlpool tubs (you can even arrange for a butler-drawn bath). Service is impeccable, and nothing has been overlooked in terms of amenities. There's an outdoor heated European-style brimming pool, where lunch is available, weather permitting, and a full-service spa. For a truly away-from-it-all feeling, consider staying at one the inn's ultraprivate riverfront Wharf Cottages ($585–1,300—ouch!), which face Dock Square from across the river. The inn also has a Hinckley Talaria-44 available for charter.

The Beach House Inn faces Middle Beach and is a bit less formal than the White Barn, but the service is on par. The Breakwater, at the mouth of the Kennebunk River, comprises a beautifully renovated, historical inn with wraparound porches and an adjacent, more modern, newly renovated building that houses rooms and a full-service spa. The complex also is home to Stripers Restaurant. Finally, there's the Yachtsman, an innovative blend of a motel and B&B, with all rooms opening onto patios facing the river and the marina where George H. W. Bush keeps his boat.

Innkeeper (and restaurateur and artist) Jack Nahil seems to have a magic touch with everything he undertakes. Now he's rehabbed the **C Cape Arundel Inn** (208 Ocean Ave., Kennebunkport, 207/967-2125, www.capearundelinn.com), making it (and its restaurant) a prime destination. The fabulous ocean view (all but two rooms overlook the Bush estate) doesn't hurt, either. The Cape Arundel compound comprises the Shingle-style main inn building (seven rooms, most with water view; $295–375 peak), the Rockbound motel-style building (six rooms with sea-view balconies; $315–375 peak), and the Carriage House Loft, a large suite on the upper floor of the carriage house ($295 peak); an expanded continental breakfast buffet is included. Most rooms have fireplaces; Rockbound and Carriage House have TV. Open March–January 1. The inn's restaurant, where every table has an ocean view, earns raves for its intriguingly creative cuisine; entrées are $20–34.

If nonstop beaching is your vacation goal, book one of the 22 rooms at **Tides Inn by-the-Sea** (252 Kings Hwy., Goose Rocks Beach, Kennebunkport, 207/967-3757, www.tidesinnbythesea.com), directly across the street from superb Goose Rocks Beach. Decor at the John Calvin Stevens–designed Victorian inn is funky, whimsical (faux painting, costumed dummies, a resident ghost named Emma), and altogether fun. Next door is **Tides Too**, a modern, condo-type building with one- and two-bedroom efficiencies by the week ($3,500 for four people). Inn rooms, early June–Labor Day, go for $195–325 d, including continental breakfast. Open mid-May–mid-October. The inn's first-rate Belvidere Club is open to the public Wednesday–Sunday for breakfast and creative dinners with a small but select menu (entrées $22–25).

The sprawling, riverfront **Nonantum Resort** (95 Ocean Ave., P.O. Box 2626, Kennebunkport 04046, 207/967-4050 or 800/552-5651, www.nonantumresort.com, $189–439) complex, which dates from 1884, includes a bit of everything, from simple rooms with an old-fashioned, Victorian decor to modern family suites with kitchenettes. Some rooms have views to the open ocean. Facilities include a dining room, outdoor heated pool and whirlpool, and docking facilities—two tour boats are based here. All 115 rooms have air-conditioning, Wi-Fi, and TV; some have refrigerators. Rates include a full breakfast. The dining room is also open for dinner and, in July and August, lunch. Packages, many of which include dinner, are a good choice. Do note: Weddings take place here almost every weekend. Open April–early December.

Innkeepers and chefs Brian and Shanna O'Hea (they met at the Culinary Institute of America) have created a lovely escape at **The Kennebunk Inn** (45 Main St., Kennebunk, 207/985-3351, www.thekennebunkinn.com, $125–160 peak), a rambling 1799 inn in downtown Kennebunk. No two rooms are alike, and renovation is an ongoing process. Some have air-conditioning or antique claw-foot tubs or fireplaces, all have Wi-Fi, TV, and phone. The

inn has both a dining room (5–9 P.M. Wed.–Sat., entrées $19–28) and pub (5–9 P.M. daily, $7–15). Rates include a continental breakfast. A few pet-friendly rooms ($20 per stay) are available.

Bed-and-Breakfasts
Three of Kennebunkport's lovliest inns are rumored to have been owned by brothers-in-law, all of whom were sea captains. Rivaling the White Barn Inn for service, decor, amenities, and overall luxury is the three-story **⊂ The Captain Lord Mansion** (P.O. Box 800, Kennebunkport 04046, 207/967-3141 or 800/522-3141, www.captainlord.com, $215–450), which is one of the finest B&Bs anywhere. And no wonder. Innkeepers Rick and Bev Litchfield have been at it since 1978, and they're never content to rest on their laurels. Each year the inn improves upon seeming perfection. If you want to be pampered and stay in a meticulously decorated and historical B&B with marble bathrooms (heated floors, many with double whirlpool tubs), fireplaces, original artwork, phones, and air-conditioning in all rooms and even a few cedar closets, then look no further. Even breakfast is a special affair, with fresh-squeezed orange juice made from oranges flown in daily. Bicycles and beach towels and chairs are available. Afternoon treats are provided.

The elegant, Federal-style **The Captain Jefferds Inn** (5 Pearl St., P.O. Box 691, Kennebunkport 04046, 207/967-2311 or 800/839-6844, www.captainjefferdsinn.com, $150–360), in the historic district, provides the ambience of a real captain's house. Each of the 15 rooms and suites (11 in the main house and four more in the carriage house) have plush linens, fresh flowers, down comforters, CD players, and air-conditioning; some have fireplaces, whirlpool tubs, and other luxuries. A three-course breakfast and afternoon tea are included.

The **Captain Fairfield Inn** (8 Pleasant St., P.O. Box 3089, Kennebunkport 04046, www.captainfairfield.com, $225–340) is perhaps the most modest architecturally of the three, but it doesn't scrimp on amenities. Innkeepers Rob and Leigh Blood are slowly replacing traditional decor with a more contemporary style. All rooms have flat-screen TVs, air-conditioning, and Wi-Fi; some have gas fireplaces. The lovely grounds are a fine place to retreat for a snooze in the hammock or a game of croquet. Rates include a four-course breakfast.

Hidden in a woodsy, private residential neighborhood, the lovely **Old Fort Inn** (Old Fort Ave., P.O. Box M, Kennebunkport 04046, 207/828-3678, www.oldfortinn.com) is the kind of place that you might not want to leave, even for touring or shopping. Once part of a Colony-style grand hotel, the stable has been renovated into elegant, spacious guest rooms, many with fireplaces and/or jetted tubs, all with wetbars equipped with fridge and microwave. The main building houses a huge common room and a screened porch. On the 15-acre premises are a heated pool, tennis court, and antiques shop. Breakfast is a lavish hot-and-cold buffet. Rates are $160–375.

The inspiration for the **English Meadows Inn** (141 Port Rd., Lower Village, Kennebunk, 207/967-5766, www.englishmeadowsinn.com, $175–305 peak) came from those lovely English manor homes, elegant yet comfortable. The 1860s original Greek Revival architecture was married to the Victorian Queen Anne style later in the century. Inside, the woodwork gleams, the floors, scattered with Asian-style rugs, shine, and the antiques and country comfort pieces mix with an unusual collection of Asian and English antiques, collected by the owner when living abroad. Books fill the inn's many nooks and crannies. Rooms are split between the main house, carriage house (where children are welcome), and a pet-friendly, two-bedroom cottage, a good choice for young families. Breakfast is elaborate.

The low-key, turn-of-the-20th-century **Green Heron Inn** (126 Ocean Ave., Kennebunkport, 207/967-3315, www.greenheroninn.com) sees many repeat guests. Ten rooms and a two-story cottage have TV, phones, air-conditioning, private baths; some have fireplace, microwave, or refrigerator; and most have cove views. Prices are $145–175 d (cottage is $250). Children are welcome; some pets are accepted ($10 per night). Also included is breakfast—one of the best in town—served in the coveside breakfast room.

Neighboring the Wedding Cake House, **The Waldo Emerson Inn** (108 Summer St., Rte. 35, Kennebunk, 207/985-4250, www.waldoemersoninn.com) has a charming colonial feel—as it should, since the main section was built in 1784. Poet Ralph Waldo Emerson spent many a summer in this, his great-uncle's home. Six attractive rooms, three with working fireplaces, are $135–150 peak, including full breakfast. In-room massages are available. Quilters, take note: In the barn is Mainely Quilts, a well-stocked quilt shop, open daily in summer.

You'll awake to the drone of lobster-boat engines at **The Inn at Harbor Head** (41 Pier Rd., Cape Porpoise, Kennebunkport, 207/967-5564, www.harborhead.com), an idyllic spot on Cape Porpoise Harbor, 2.5 miles from Dock Square. Hand-painted murals, monogrammed bathrobes, flower bouquets, a superb library, hammocks in the yard, Wi-Fi, and outstanding views are just a few of the many pluses here. It offers three rooms and one good-size suite, some with whirlpool tub, fireplace, or private deck. Rates are $195–325 d.

Here's a bargain: The nonprofit **Franciscan Guest House** (28 Beach Ave., P.O. Box 980, Kennebunkport 04046, 207/967-4865, www.franciscanguesthouse.com), on the grounds of the monastery, has accommodations spread among two buildings, as well as three other Tudor-style cottages. Accommodations are basic, but they do have some nice amenities, including TV, air-conditioning, saltwater pool, and beach passes. A buffet breakfast is included in the rates, and a buffet dinner often is available. There is no daily mail service, but fresh towels are provided daily. Rooms are $92–154, and one- to three-bedroom suites are $149–279. No credit cards.

Motels and Cottages

Patricia Mason is the 12th-generation innkeeper at **⊂ The Seaside Motor Inn and**

Cottages (80 Beach Ave., Kennebunk, mailing address P.O. Box 631, Kennebunkport 04046, 207/967-4461 or 800/967-4461 www.kennebunkbeach.com, $229–249), a property that has been in her family since the mid-1600s. What a location! The 22-room motel and 10 cottages sit on 20 acres bordered by the Atlantic Ocean, the Kennebec River, and Gooch's River. It's the only truly beachfront property in the area, with a private beach for guests. Motel rooms are spacious, with TV, air-conditioning, and refrigerators. A continental breakfast is included in the rates. The one- to four-bedroom cottages are rented by the week early and late season and by the month in July and August.

With indoor and outdoor heated pools and whirlpools and a good-size fitness center, the **Rhumb Line Motor Lodge** (Ocean Ave., P.O. Box 3067, Kennebunkport 04046, 207/967-5457 or 800/337-4862, www.rhumblinemaine.com) is a magnet for families. This well-managed two-story establishment in a quiet residential area three miles from Dock Square has easy access to the trolley-bus service. Fifty-nine large rooms have private balcony or patio, phones, air-conditioning, Wi-Fi, cable TV, and small refrigerators. Free continental breakfast. From late May to mid-September, weather permitting, there are nightly poolside lobster bakes. Rates are $155–185; kids 12 and under stay free. Closed in January.

Compared with other intown properties, the **Fontenay Terrace Motel** (128 Ocean Ave., Kennebunkport, 207/967-3556, www.fontenaymotel.com, $140–175 peak) is a bargain. Second-generation innkeepers David and Paula Reid keep the place spotless. It borders a tidal inlet and has a private grassy and shaded lawn, perfect for retreating from the hubbub of busy Kennebunkport. Each of the eight rooms has air-conditioning, minifridge, microwave, Wi-Fi, cable TV, and phone; some have water views. A small beach is 300 yards away, and it's a pleasant one-mile walk to Dock Square.

The clean and simple **Cape Porpoise Motel** (12 Mills Rd., Rte. 9, P.O. Box 7218, Cape Porpoise 04014, 207/967-3370, www.capeporpoisemotel.com, $125–150 peak) is a short walk from the harbor. All rooms have TV and air-conditioning, some have kitchenettes; rates include a continental breakfast, with muffins, fruit, and other surprises. Also available by the week or month are efficiencies with full kitchens, phones, and one or more bedrooms.

FOOD

Hours are for peak season, when reservations are advised. Call ahead September–June.

Local Flavors

All Day Breakfast (55 Western Ave., Rte. 9, Lower Village, Kennebunk, 207/967-5132) is a favorite meeting spot, offering such specialties as invent-your-own omelettes and crepes, Texas French toast, and the ADB sandwich. ADB is open 7 A.M.–1:30 P.M. weekdays in summer (to 2 P.M. weekends). Closed mid-December–mid-January.

It's hard to choose the perfect pastry from the large selection at **Port Bakery and Café** (181 Port Rd., Kennebunk, 207/967-2263, opens at 7 A.M. daily). Hot breakfasts are also available, as are soups and sandwiches and other goodies. Eat in or outside on the deck or take it all to go.

Conveniently near the Kennebunk and Kennebunkport Chamber of Commerce, **H. B. Provisions** (15 Western Ave., Lower Village, Kennebunk, 207/967-5762) has an excellent wine selection, along with plenty of picnic supplies, newspapers, and all the typical general-store inventory. It also serves breakfast and prepares hot and cold sandwiches, salads, and wraps. It's open daily all year.

The name says it all at **The Bakery and Café** (50 Main St., Kennebunk, 207/985-7888, 6 A.M.–6 P.M. daily and 5–8 P.M. Fri.), a bright and airy downtown spot. Soups, salads, sandwiches, fancy coffees, and pastries are the usuals, but it's also open Friday nights for pizza and stromboli.

Equal parts fancy food and wine store and gourmet café, **Cape Porpoise Kitchen** (Rte. 9, Cape Porpoise, 207/967-1150, 7 A.M.–7 P.M.

daily) sells sandwiches, salads, prepared foods, desserts, and everything to go with.

While away an afternoon with a traditional English tea at the **English Meadows Inn** (141 Port Rd., Lower Village, Kennebunk, 207/967-5766, 2–4 P.M. Thurs.–Sat.). Choose from a cream tea ($12.95), with tea, scones, and sweets, or a Queen's tea ($19.95), which adds petite sandwiches to the tray. It's beautifully presented, served in a lovely room or perhaps the garden. Reservations required.

The **Kennebunk Farmers Market** sets up shop mid-May–mid-October in the Grove Street municipal parking lot off Route 1 (behind the Mobil station). Hours are 8 A.M.–noon Saturday. Vendors sell crafts, condiments, fresh produce (including organic), flowers, breads, biscotti; special events (tastings, etc.) are sometimes on the agenda.

Family Favorites

The nearest thing to being afloat is sitting at a riverfront deck table at **Arundel Wharf** (43 Ocean Ave., Kennebunkport, 207/967-3444), where passing tour and lobster boats provide lunchtime entertainment. Captain's chairs and chart-topped tables complete the nautical picture. Burgers and fries are always on the menu for kids; adults might want to limit their choices to similar fare—dinner entrées are $14–30. Open at 11:30 A.M. daily for lunch and dinner mid-May–mid-December; reservations are wise for dinner.

A bit off the beaten track is **Lucas on 9** (62 Mills Rd./Rte. 9, Cape Porpoise, 207/967-0039, www.lucason9.com), a family-friendly, family-operated restaurant, and the Lane family knows food. Chef Jonathan Lane makes everything from scratch and delivers on his mother Deborah's mission of "Good American food at affordable prices." Jonathan's travels have infused his preparations with more than a bow toward his work on Southern riverboats (Louisiana spicy crab soup, bread pudding with whisky). There are at least six specials nightly in addition to plenty of other choices ($13–30). The restaurant is named for Jonathan's brother Lucas, who died in 2005. It's

open 11:30 A.M.–9 P.M., closed Tuesday and mid-December–early April.

Grab a stool at the counter, slip into a booth, or wait for a table at the **Wayfarer** (Pier Rd., Cape Porpoise, 207/967-8961), a casual restaurant that serves breakfast, lunch, and dinner to locals and in-the-know tourists (dinner entrées $10–19). It's open 7 A.M.–12:30 P.M. and 5–8 P.M. Tuesday–Saturday and 7 A.M.–noon Sunday. Good lobster stew; nightly dinner specials. Most choices are in the $10–19 range. No credit cards.

Casual Dining

Brian and Shanna O'Hea met at the Culinary Institute of America, and they've had a fine time creating **Academe** (The Kennebunk Inn, 45 Main St., Kennebunk, 207/985-3351, www.kennebunkinn.com), which they bill as a Maine brasserie and tavern. The choices vary from panini and pizzas to cashew-crusted wild salmon, which puts it within most budgets. The lunch menu, served Monday–Friday, comprises mostly soups and salads. A full dinner menu is served Tuesday–Saturday; a limited menu on Sunday and Monday. Children's menu selections are $4.50.

Just west of the junction of Routes 9 and 35 is the casually elegant **Grissini Trattoria** (27 Western Ave., Kennebunk, 207/967-2211, 5:30–9 P.M., Fri. and Sat. to 9:30 P.M.), a sibling of the White Barn Inn. Attentive service, an inspired Tuscan menu (entrées $15–33), and a bright, open-beamed space make it an appealing spot. In nice weather, try for the sunken patio.

The views complement the food at **Hurricane Restaurant** (29 Dock Sq., Kennebunkport, 207/967-9111, www.hurricanerestaurant.com), where the dining room hangs over the river. A longtime favorite in Ogunquit, this is now the only location, but it continues to reel in the crowds, both for location and for quality and creativity. Dinner entrées begin at $19.

Eat well and feel good about it at **Bandaloop** (2 Dock Sq., Kennebunkport, 207/967-4994, www.bandaloop.biz, 5:30–9:30 P.M. daily), a hip, vibrant restaurant where chef/owner

W. Scott Lee likes to push boundaries. Lee named the restaurant for author Tom Robbins's fictional tribe that knew the secret to eternal life. Lee believes the secret is fresh, local, organic, and cruelty free. Selections vary from meats and fish to vegetarian and vegan ($14–24); pair a "center of plate selection" with one of eight sauces, choose from nightly specials, or simply make a meal from the appetizers.

Fancy to Fine Dining

Every table at the **Cape Arundel Inn** (208 Ocean Ave., Kennebunkport, 207/967-2125, www.capearundelinn.com) has a knockout view of crashing surf, and the food matches the view. White-clothed tables topped with cobalt blue glassware add to the inn's casual yet elegant feel. Local artwork covers the walls. Chef Rich Lemoine's menu emphasizes fish and seafood in classic preparations, all prepared and served with care. Prices range from high $20s to mid $30s. Open for dinner daily (closed Mon. off season).

Floor-to-ceiling windows frame the Kennebunk River breakwater, providing perfect views for those indulging at **Stripers** (at the Breakwater Inn, 127 Ocean Ave., Kennebunkport, 207/967-5333), another White Barn Inn sibling. The emphasis on fish is also accented by a saltwater tank with coral reef and exotic fish. It's no surprise that fish and seafood are the specialties, with most entrées in the $18–28 range. Dress is casual. Valet parking is available. It's open 5:30–9 P.M., to 9:30 P.M. Friday and Saturday, April–late October, also 11:30 A.M.–2 P.M. Memorial Day–Labor Day.

Fusion cuisine reigns at **On the Marsh** (46 Western Ave./Rte. 9, Lower Village, Kennebunk, 207/967-2299, www.onthemarsh.com), a restored barn overlooking marshlands leading to Kennebunk Beach. Entrée range is $21–35. The decor here is astonishing, courtesy of owner Denise Rubin, an interior designer: raspberry exterior and art and antiques on both floors of the interior. Dining choices include both an "owner's table" and a "kitchen table." Entrées might include grilled tuna with French bean salad and

seared sea scallops with lobster risotto. Quiet piano music adds to the elegant but unstuffy ambience; service is attentive. Reservations are essential in midsummer. It's open for dinner 5:30–9:30 P.M. daily. Closed January.

Winner of a raft of culinary awards, **Windows on the Water** (12 Chase Hill Rd., Kennebunk 04043, 207/967-3313 or 800/773-3313, www.windowsonthewater.com, 11:30 A.M.–2:30 P.M. and 5:30–9:30 P.M., to 10:30 P.M. Fri. and Sat.) has been filling its screened porch, patio, and dining rooms since 1985. It's appropriately named, with big windows providing views over nearby shops to the busy harbor. Lunch entrées are $9–17; dinner entrées are $19–39, the high end for such dishes as lobster ravioli and Thai lobster; and the White Porch Bistro (opens for dinner at 5 P.M.) serves pub-style fare. Best deals are the five-course lunch for $15 and the three-course dinner for $33; add $10 for a bottle of wine. Reservations are advisable—essential in midsummer.

Both the view and the food are outstanding at **Pier 77** (77 Pier Rd., Cape Porpoise, 207/967-8500, 11:30 A.M.–2:30 P.M. and 5–9 P.M. daily). Chef Peter and his wife, Kate, have created an especially welcoming restaurant, where the menu varies from duck three ways to seafood mixed grill (entrées $16–30). Frequent live entertainment provides nice background and complements the views over Cape Porpoise Harbor, with lobster boats hustling to and fro. Reservations are advisable. Practically hidden downstairs is **The Ramp Bar and Grille** (11:30 A.M.–10 P.M. daily), with lighter fare and a sports-pub decor.

Destination Dining

One of Maine's biggest splurges is **The White Barn Inn** (37 Beach Ave., Kennebunkport, 207/967-2321, www.whitebarninn.com, 6–9 P.M. Mon.–Thurs., 5:30–9:15 P.M. Fri.–Sun.), with haute cuisine, haute prices, haute-rustic barn. In summer, don't be surprised to run into members of the senior George Bush clan (probably at the back window table). Soft piano music accompanies impeccable service and chef Jonathan Carter's outstanding four-course fixed-price menu ($92 pp, excluding wine). Reservations are essential—well ahead during July and August—and you'll need a credit card (cancel 24 hours ahead or you'll have a charge). No jeans or sneakers—jackets are required. It's New England's only four-star, five-diamond, Relais Gourmand restaurant. Closed early–late January.

Lobster and Clams

Nunan's Lobster Hut (9 Mills Rd., Cape Porpoise, 207/967-4362, 5 P.M.–close daily) is an institution. Sure, other places might have better views, but this casual dockside eatery with indoor and outdoor seating has been serving lobsters since 1953.

Adjacent to the bridge connecting Kennebunkport's Dock Square to Kennebunk's Lower Village is another time-tested classic, the **Clam Shack** (Rte. 9, Kennebunkport, 207/967-2560, www.theclamshack.net). The tiny take-out stand serves perhaps the state's best lobster rolls, jam-packed with meat and available with either butter or mayo, and dee-lish fried clams. It opens at 11 A.M. daily May–October for lunch and dinner.

Bush-watchers often head to **Mabel's Lobster Claw** (Ocean Ave., Kennebunkport, 207/967-2562, 11:30 A.M.–3 P.M. and 5–9 P.M. daily), hoping to spot the former president (the little place is just around the corner from Walker's Point). Try Mabel Hanson's chowder or a lobster roll and see why the restaurant's a favorite (entrées top off around $30); reservations are wise.

INFORMATION AND SERVICES
Information

The Kennebunk and Kennebunkport Chamber of Commerce (17 Western Ave., Rte. 9, Lower Village, P.O. Box 740, Kennebunk 04043, 207/967-0857, www.visitthekennebunks.com) produces an excellent area guide to accommodations, restaurants, area maps, bike maps, tide calendars, recreation, and beach parking permits.

Check out Louis T. Graves Memorial Public Library (18 Maine St., Kennebunkport, 207/967-2778, www.graves.lib.me.us) or Kennebunk Free Library (112 Main St., 207/985-2173, kennebunklibrary.org).

Public Restrooms

Public toilets are at Gooch's and Mother's Beaches and at St. Anthony's Monastery, the chamber of commerce building (17 Western Ave.), and at the chamber's Dock Square Hospitality Center.

GETTING THERE AND AROUND

Amtrak's **Downeaster** (800/872-7245, www.thedowneaster.com) connects Boston's North Station with Portland, Maine, with stops in Wells, Saco, and Old Orchard Beach (seasonal).

Vermont Transit (800/552-8737, www.vermonttransit.com), a division of Greyhound bus lines, stops at the Wells Regional Transportation Center daily on the Boston–Portland–Bangor route. The trolley connects with the bus in season and stops in Kennebunk's Lower Village.

From Memorial Day to mid-October, the **Intown Trolley** (207/967-3686, www.intowntrolley.com) operates a 45-minute narrated sightseeing tour throughout Kennebunk and Kennebunkport, originating in Dock Square and making regular stops at beaches and other attractions. The entire route takes about 45 minutes, with the driver providing a hefty dose of local history and gossip. Seats are park bench–style. An all-day ticket is $13 adults, $6 children 3–14. You can get on or off at any stop. The trolley operates hourly 10 A.M.–5 P.M. in July and August, to 4 P.M. in spring and fall.

The free **Shoreline Explorer Kennebunk Shuttle** (www.shorelineexplorer.com) circulates hourly between Grove Street parking lot, Stop and Shop, Landing Store, Lower Village, and the beaches 10 A.M.–10:30 P.M. late June–Labor Day. It connects with the Shoreline and Intown trolleys.

Old Orchard Beach Area

Seven continuous miles of white sand beach has been drawing vacation-oriented folks for generations to the area stretching from Camp Ellis, in Saco, to Pine Point, in Scarborough. Cottage colonies and condo complexes dominate at the extremities, but the center of activity has always been and remains Old Orchard Beach.

In its heyday, Old Orchard Beach's pier reached far out into the sea, huge resort hotels lined the sands, and wealthy Victorian folk (including Rose Fitzgerald and Joe Kennedy, who met on these sands in the days when men strolled around in dress suits and women toted parasols) came each summer to see and be seen.

Storms and fires have taken their toll through the years, and the grand resorts have been replaced by endless motels, many of which display *Nous parlons Français* signs to welcome the masses of French Canadians who arrive each summer. They're accompanied by young families, who come for the sand and surf, and T-shirted and body-pierced young pleasure seekers, who come for the nightlife. (You'd better like people if you stop here, because this town welcomes tourists—the population expands from about 8,000 in winter to about 100,000 in midsummer.)

Although some residents are pushing gentrification, and a few projects are pushing it in that direction, Old Orchard Beach remains somewhat honky-tonk, and most of its visitors would have it no other way. French fries, cotton candy, and beach-accessories shops line the downtown, and as you get closer to the pier, you pass arcades and amusement parks. There's not a kid on earth who wouldn't have fun in Old Orchard—even if some parents might find it all a bit much.

Much more sedate are the villages on the fringes. The **Ocean Park** section of Old Orchard, at the southwestern end of town, was established in 1881 as a religious summer-cottage community. It still offers interdenominational services and vacation Bible school, but it also

has an active cultural association that sponsors concerts, Chautauqua-type lectures, films, and other events throughout the summer. All are open to the public.

South of that is **Camp Ellis.** Begun as a small fishing village named after early settler Thomas Ellis, Camp Ellis is crowded with longtime summer homes that are in a constant battle with the sea. A nearly mile-long granite jetty—designed to keep silt from clogging the Saco River—has taken the blame for massive beach erosion since constructed. But the jetty is a favorite spot for wetting a line (no fishing license needed) and for panoramic views off toward Wood Island Light (built in 1808) and Biddeford Pool. Camp Ellis Beach is open to the public, with lifeguards on duty in midsummer. Parking—scarce on hot days—is $10 a day.

As you head north from Old Orchard you'll pass **Pine Point,** another longtime community of vacation homes. Services are few and parking is $10 a day.

Most folks get to Old Orchard by passing through **Saco** and **Biddeford,** which have long been upstairs/downstairs sister cities, with wealthy mill owners living in Saco and their workers (and workplaces) in Biddeford. But even those personalities have always been split—congested, commercial Route 1 is part of Saco, and the exclusive enclave of Biddeford Pool is, of course, in below-stairs Biddeford. Saco still has an attractive downtown, with boutiques and stunning homes on Main Street and beyond.

Blue-collar Biddeford is working hard to change its milltown image. It's home to the magnificent Biddeford City Theater and the University of New England, and as a Main Street community, it's getting a much-needed sprucing up. New shops and restaurants are balancing the numerous thrift shops downtown, and artisans and woodworkers are filling vacant mills. Another Biddeford hallmark is its Franco American tradition—thanks to the French-speaking workers who sustained the textile and shoemaking industries in the 19th century. Never is the heritage more evident than during Biddeford's annual La Kermesse festival in late June.

SIGHTS

Founded in 1866, the **Saco Museum** (371 Main St., Saco, 207/283-3861, www.dyerlibrarysacomuseum.org, noon–4 P.M. Tues.–Sun., to 8 P.M. Thurs., $4 adults, $3 seniors, $2 students) rotates selections from its outstanding collection, including 18th- and 19th-century paintings, furniture, and other household treasures. Lectures, workshops, and concerts are also part of the annual schedule. Admission is free after 4 P.M. Thursday.

PARKS AND PRESERVES

Saco Bay Trails, a local land trust, has produced a very helpful trail guide that includes the Saco Heath, the East Point Sanctuary, and more than a dozen other local trails. The Cascade Falls trail, for example, is a half-mile stroll ending at a waterfall. Copies are available for $5 at a number of Biddeford and Saco locations (including the Dyer Library) or from Saco Bay Trails (P.O. Box 7505, Ocean Park 04063). Trail information is also on the organization's website: www.sacobaytrails.org.

◖ East Point Sanctuary

Owned by Maine Audubon, the 30-acre East Point Sanctuary is a splendid preserve at the eastern end of Biddeford Pool. Crashing surf, beach roses, bayberry bushes, and offshore Wood Island Light are all features of the two-part perimeter trail here—skirting the golf course of the exclusive Abenakee Club. Allow at least an hour; even in fog, the setting is dramatic. During spring and fall migrations, it's one of southern Maine's prime birding locales, so you'll have plenty of company if you show up then, and the usual streetside parking may be scarce. It's open sunrise–sundown all year. It's poorly signposted (perhaps deliberately?), so here are the directions: From Route 9 (Main St.) in downtown Biddeford, take Route 9/208 (Pool Rd.) southeast about five miles to the

Route 208 turnoff to Biddeford Pool. Go 0.6 mile on Route 208 (Bridge Rd.), and then left onto Mile Stretch Road. Continue to Lester B. Orcutt Boulevard, turn left, and go to the end. For further information, contact Maine Audubon (20 Gilsland Farm Rd., P.O. Box 6009, Falmouth 04105, 207/781-2330).

The Heath

Owned by The Nature Conservancy, 870-acre **Saco Heath Preserve** is the nation's southernmost "raised coalesced bog," where peat accumulated through eons into two above-water dome shapes that eventually merged into a single natural feature. For a bit of esoterica, it's the home of the rare Hessel's hairstreak butterfly. Pick up a map at the parking area and follow the mile-long, self-guided trail through the woods and then into the heath via a boardwalk. Best time to come is early–mid-October, when the heath and woodland colors are positively brilliant and insects are on the wane. You're likely to see deer and perhaps even spot a moose. The preserve entrance is on Route 112, Buxton Road, two miles west of I-95. Open all year, sunrise–sunset, it's also popular with snowshoers and cross-country skiers in winter.

Ferry Beach State Park

When the weather's hot, arrive early at Ferry Beach State Park (Bay View Rd., off Rte. 9, Saco, 207/283-0067, $3 adults, $1 children 5–11, free for seniors and kids under 5), a pristine beach backed by dune grass on Saco Bay. In the 117-acre park are changing rooms, restrooms, lifeguard, picnic tables, and five easy interconnected nature trails winding through woodlands, marshlands, and dunes. (Later in the day, keep the insect repellent handy.) It's open daily, late May–late September, but accessible all year. (Trail markers are removed in winter.)

RECREATION
Golf

Opened in 1922 as a nine-hole course, the **Biddeford-Saco Country Club** (101 Old Or-

AMUSEMENT PARKS AND AMUSING PLACES

If you've got kids or just love amusement parks, you'll find Maine's best in the Old Orchard area, where sand and sun just seem to complement arcades and rides perfectly.

The biggie is **Funtown/Splashtown USA** (774 Portland Rd., Rte. 1, Saco, 207/284-5139 or 800/878-2900, www.funtownsplashtownusa.com). Ride Maine's only wooden roller coaster; fly down New England's longest and tallest log flume ride; free fall 200 feet on Dragon's Descent; get wet and go wild riding speed slides, tunnel slides, raft slides, and river slides or splashing in the pool. Add a huge kiddie ride section, games, food, and other activities for a full day or family fun. Funtown opens weekends in early May, Splashtown in mid-June; everything's up and running daily late June–Labor Day, when Funtown is open 10 A.M.–9 P.M., to 10 P.M. Saturday, and Splashtown 10 A.M.–6 P.M. Rates vary by height, with Big for those 48 inches and taller, Little for those 38–48 inches tall and seniors, and free for kids less than 38 inches tall. A Funtown USA Ride Pass provides two rides on the Grand Prix Racers and unlimited use of all other rides for $25 Big, $17 Little, and a night special valid after 5 P.M. is $18 Big and $12 Little. A Splashtown unlimited slide pass is $20 Big and $17 Little. Combo passes for two rides on the Grand Prix Racers and unlimited use of all other rides, slides, and pools, is $34 Big and $25 Little. Season passes also are available.

Three miles north of Funtown/ Splashtown USA, **Aquaboggan Water Park** (980 Portland Rd., Rte. 1, Saco, 207/282-3112, www.aquabogganwaterpark.com) is wet and wild, with such stomach turners as the Yankee Ripper, the Suislide, and the Stealth, with an almost-vertical drop of 45 feet – enough to accelerate to 30 mph on the descent. Wear a bathing suit that won't abandon you in the rough-and-tumble. Also, if you wear glasses, safety straps and plastic lenses are required. Besides all the water stuff, there are shuffleboard courts, minigolf, an arcade, picnic tables, and snack bars. Lots of ticket options cover varying numbers of attractions. You can pay as you go, one attraction at a time, but it adds up quickly; Mondays and Fridays are $10 for the day. It's open 10 A.M.–6 P.M. daily late June–Labor Day.

The biggest beachfront amusement park, **Palace Playland** (1 Old Orchard St., Old Orchard, 207/934-2001, www.palaceplayland.com) has more than 25 rides and attractions packed into four acres, including a giant water slide, fun house, bumper cars, Ferris wheel, roller coaster, and a 24,000-square-foot arcade with more than 200 games. For a bird's-eye view of the area, ride the 75-foot-high gondola Sunwheel. Get soaked riding the Log Flume. Rev up the action on two roller coasters, one with a five-story drop, both with high-speed twisting turns. Kiddie Land has more than a dozen rides, including a fun house and a splashing whale. An unlimited pass is $26.50 per day; a kiddie pass good for all two-ticket rides is $19.50; two-day, season, and per ride tickets ($2-4) are available. Open Memorial Day–Labor Day.

The Old Orchard Pier, jutting 475 feet into the ocean from downtown, is a minimall of shops, arcades, and fast-food outlets. Far longer when it was built in 1898, it's been lopped off gradually by fires and storms. The current incarnation has been here since the late 1970s.

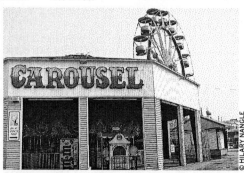

© HILARY NANGLE

Old-time amusements are still a big draw in Old Orchard Beach.

chard Rd., Saco, 207/282-5883) added a back nine in 1987 (toughest hole on the par-71 course is the 11th). Tee times not usually needed. Fees are moderate.

Covering more than 300 acres is the challenging 18-hole, par-71 **Dunegrass Golf Club** (200 Wild Dunes Way, Old Orchard Beach, 207/934-4513 or 800/521-1029). Greens fees are a bit steep, but well worth a splurge. Tee times are essential. The sprawling modern clubhouse has a restaurant and pro shop.

Sea Kayaking
Gone with the Wind (Yates St., Biddeford Pool, 207/283-8446, www.gwtwonline.com) offers two tours, afternoon and sunset, with prices varying with the number of people on the tour (two people are about $85 pp). Wetsuits are supplied. The most popular trip is to Beach Island. Also available are rentals ($40 half day, $60 full day). Kids and seniors get a $10 pp discount.

Surfing
A seasonal branch of **Aquaholics Surf Shop** (www.aquaholicsurf.com) rents surfboards, bodyboards, wetsuits, and related gear from a kiosk next to the pier and Palace Playland.

ENTERTAINMENT
Biddeford City Theater
Designed by noted architect John Calvin Stevens in 1896, the 500-seat National Historic Register Biddeford City Theater (205 Main St., P.O. Box 993, Biddeford 04005, 207/282-0849, www.citytheater.org) has been superbly restored, and acoustics are excellent even when Eva Gray, the resident ghost, mixes it up backstage. A respected community theater group mounts a winter drama season and showcases other talent throughout the year. Check local papers or call for schedule.

Fireworks
Fireworks are set off by the pier in Old Orchard Beach at 9:45 P.M. every Thursday late June–Labor Day.

Live Music and Performances
You'll find plenty of it in Old Orchard Beach at places including **Pier Patio Pub, Village Inn, PICS Pizza,** and **Surf 6.** In Biddeford, there's live music at **Bebe's Burritos** (140 Main St., 207/283-4222, www.bebesburritos.com) 7–10:30 P.M. every Thursday, Friday, and Saturday.

Free concerts are staged by the pier at 7 P.M. every Monday and Tuesday in July and August.

Another option for family concerts and other performances is the **Old Orchard Beach Pavilion** (Union Ave. and 6th St., 207/934-2024, www.oobpavilion.org).

Ocean Park's **Temple,** a 19th-century octagon that seats 800-plus, is the venue for Sunday-night concerts (7:30 P.M., $8 adults) and many other programs throughout the summer.

EVENTS
La Kermesse (meaning the fair or the festival) is Biddeford's summer highlight, when nearly 50,000 visitors pour into town on the last full weekend in June (Thurs.–Sun.) to celebrate the town's Franco American heritage. Local volunteers go all out to plan block parties, a parade, games, carnival, live entertainment, and traditional dancing—most of it centered on Biddeford's Waterhouse Field. Then there's *la cuisine franco-américaine;* you can fill up on *boudin, creton, poutine, tourtière, tarte au saumon,* and crepes (although your arteries may rebel).

Generally scheduled for the Saturday of the same weekend, the **Saco Sidewalk Arts Festival** involves more than 150 artists exhibiting their work all along Saco's Main Street. Strolling musicians, kids' activities, and food booths are all part of the well-organized, daylong event.

In July, the parishioners of St. Demetrios Greek Orthodox Church (186 Bradley St., Saco, 207/284-5651) go all out to mount the annual **Greek Heritage Festival,** a three-day extravaganza of homemade Greek food, traditional Greek music and dancing, and a craft fair. Be sure to tour the impressive $1.5 million domed church building.

Football fans might want to watch the annual **Shriner's Lobster Bowl,** an all-star high school football game to benefit Shriner's Hospitals for Children.

The beaches come to life in July. Early July brings the annual **parade and Sandcastle Contest** to Ocean Park.

One weekend in mid-August, Old Orchard Beach's **Beach Olympics** is a family festival of games, exhibitions, and music benefiting Maine's Special Olympics program.

ACCOMMODATIONS

The area has hundreds of beds—mostly in motel-style lodgings. The chamber of commerce is the best resource for motels, cottages, and the area's more than 3,000 campsites. Only recently have a few B&Bs popped up.

The Old Orchard Beach Inn (6 Portland Ave., Old Orchard Beach, 207/934-5834 or 877/700-6624, fax 207/934-0782, www.old-orchardbeachinn.com, $110–185) was rescued from ruin by owner Steve Cecchetti and opened in summer 2000. Built in 1730, and most recently known as the Staples Inn, the National Historic Register building seemed destined for the wrecker's ball in 1997. Now it's been transformed, with 18 antiques-filled rooms with air-conditioning, phones, and TV. Continental breakfast is included in the rates; a two-bedroom suite is $250–400. Open all year.

Practically next door is **The Atlantic Birches Inn** (20 Portland Ave., Rte. 98, P.O. Box 334, Old Orchard Beach 04064, 207/934-5295 or 888/934-5295), with 10 guest rooms with air-conditioning in a Victorian house and separate cottage. Breakfast is hearty continental, and there's a swimming pool. The beach is an easy walk. Rates run $101–131 d. It's open all year, but call ahead off-season.

Look out to sea from the porch or deck of **Cristina's Bed and Breakfast** (36 Main Ave., Camp Ellis Beach, Saco, 207/282-7483, trahan@ prexar.com, $75–135), Cristina and Paul Trahan's vintage gingerbread-trimmed cottage with three pleasant guest rooms (one with private bath), all with Victorian furnishings. Rates include continental breakfast. No credit cards.

Brand spanking new and adjacent to the pier is the **Grand Victorian** (1 East Grand Ave., Old Orchard Beach, 207/934-0759, www.grandvictorianwaterfront.com), with oceanfront condominiums available for the week. Rates begin around $2,000 for a one-bedroom sleeping five. On-site are an indoor heated pool, fitness room, sauna, and spa.

FOOD
Old Orchard Beach

Dining is not Old Orchard's strong point. Nicest (although service and quality are inconsistent) is **Joseph's by the Sea** (55 W. Grand Ave., Old Orchard Beach, 207/934-5044, www.josephsbythesea.com, 7–11 A.M. and 5–9 P.M. daily), a quiet, shorefront restaurant amid all the hoopla. Request a table on the screened patio. The menu—French with a dash of Maine—has entrées in the $18–30 range. Reservations advisable in midsummer.

Immerse yourself in a Victorian manor at **Landmark** (28 E. Grand Ave., Old Orchard Beach, 207/934-0156, 5–8 P.M., to 9 P.M. Fri. and Sat.). Ornate tin ceilings, shining wood floors, and paintings distinguish the dining areas, which include an enclosed porch. Entrées ($19–22) vary from Parmesan haddock to lacquered duck; a kid's menu is available. Early-bird specials are served until 6 P.M.

Camp Ellis

Two well-seasoned family restaurants service Camp Ellis. **Wormwood's Restaurant** (16 Bay Ave., Camp Ellis Beach, Saco, 207/282-9679, 11:30 A.M.–9 P.M.), next to the stone jetty, still draws the crowds and keeps its loyal clientele happy with ample portions and $6–16 entrées. Cajun-style seafood is a specialty.

At **Huot's Seafood Restaurant** (Camp Ellis Beach, Saco, 207/282-1642, www.huotsseafoodrestaurant.com, 11 A.M.–9 P.M. Tues.–Sun.), portions are large, prices are not.

Saco

Craving fast-ish food? The Camire family operates Maine's best home-grown option, **Rapid Ray's** (189 Main St., 207/283-4222, www.rapidrays.biz,

11 A.M.–12:30 A.M. Mon.–Thurs., to 1:30 A.M. Fri. and Sat., and noon–10 P.M. Sun.). Burgers, dogs, and fried foods are the specialty at the standing-room only joint.

For more leisurely dining, book a reservation at **Mia's** (17 Pepperell Square, Saco, 207/284-6427, www.miasatpepperellsquare.com, 11 A.M.–2 P.M. and 5:30–9:30 P.M. Tues.–Sat., 9 A.M.–2 P.M. Sun.), where chef-owner Steve Rogers prepares classic fare without fuss. Dinner entrées, such as filet mignon and seared duck breast, run $17–25.

Biddeford/Biddeford Pool

For a town grounded in Franco American culture, Biddeford has an expanding array of ethnic choices, including a few that garner praise far beyond city limits: **Jewel of India** (26 Alfred St., 207/282-5600), the Vietnamese **Que Huong** (49 Main St., 207/571-8050), **Thai Siam** (144 Main St., 207/294-3300), and **Bebe's Burritos** (140 Main St., 207/283-4222), all serving lunch and dinner.

Buffleheads (122 Hills Beach Rd., 207/284-6000, www.buffleheadsrestaurant.com) is a family dining find with spectacular ocean views. Ray and Karen Wieczoreck opened the restaurant in 1994 and have built a strong local following through the years. The kids can munch on pizza, burgers, spaghetti, and other favorites while adults savor well-prepared seafood with a homestyle spin or landlubber classics. Lobster pie and a turkey dinner with all the trimmings are both perennial favorites here. Prices range $6–25. It's open 11:30 A.M.–2 P.M. and 5–8:30 P.M. daily, closed Monday off-season. Hills Beach Road branches off Route 9 at the University of New England campus.

Take your lobster or fried seafood dinner to an oceanfront picnic table on the grassy lawn behind **F. O. Goldthwaite's** (3 Lester B. Orcott Blvd., Biddeford Pool, 207/284-8872, 11 A.M.–7:30 P.M. daily), an old-fashioned general store. Salads, fried seafood, sandwiches (grilled salmon BLT!), and kid-friendly fare round out the menu ($3–15).

INFORMATION AND SERVICES

Sources of tourist information are Biddeford-Saco Chamber of Commerce and Industry (110 Main St., Saco 04072, 207/282-1567, fax 207/282-3149, www.biddefordsacochamber.org), Old Orchard Beach Chamber of Commerce (1st St., P.O. Box 600, Old Orchard Beach 04064, 207/934-2500 or 800/365-9386, www.oldorchardbeachmaine.com), and Ocean Park Association (P.O. Box 7296, Ocean Park 04063, 207/934-9068, www.oceanpark.org).

The Dyer Library (371 Main St., Saco 04072, 207/282-3031, www.sacomuseum.org), next door to the Saco Museum, attracts scads of genealogists to its vast Maine history collection. Also check out Libby Memorial Library (Staples St., Old Orchard Beach, 207/934-4351, www.ooblibrary.org).

GETTING THERE

Amtrak's **Downeaster** (800/872-7245, www.thedowneaster.com) connects Boston's North Station with Portland, Maine, with stops in Wells, Saco, and Old Orchard Beach (seasonal).

GETTING AROUND
Bus and Trolley

The **Biddeford-Saco-Old Orchard Beach Transit Committee** (207/282-5408, www.shuttlebus-zoom.com) operates three systems that make getting around simple. Between late June and Labor Day, the **Old Orchard Beach Trolley** operates on a regular schedule, connecting restaurants and campgrounds. Service begins at 10 A.M. and ends at midnight. Cost is $1 per ride; children under five ride free. **ShuttleBus Tri-Town Service** provides frequent weekday and less-frequent weekend service (except national holidays) between Biddeford, Saco, and Old Orchard Beach. One-way fare is $1.25 ages five and older, exact change required. **ShuttleBus InterCity Service** connects Biddeford, Saco, and Old Orchard with Portland, South Portland, and Scarborough. Fares vary by zones, topping at $5 for anyone over five.

GREATER PORTLAND

Whenever national magazines have articles highlighting the 10 best places to live, Greater Portland often makes the list. The very reasons that make the area so popular with residents make it equally attractive to visitors. Small in size, but big in heart, Greater Portland entices visitors with the staples—lighthouses, lobster, and L. L. Bean—but wows them with everything else it offers. It's the state's cultural hub, with performing arts centers, numerous festivals, and varied museums; a dining destination, with nationally recognized chefs as well as an amazing assortment and variety of everyday restaurants; and despite its urban environment, it has a mind-boggling amount of recreational opportunities.

Portland's population hovers around 65,000, but when the suburbs are included, it climbs to nearly a quarter of a million souls, making it Maine's largest, by far. Take a swing through the bedroom communities of Scarborough, Cape Elizabeth, and South Portland, and you'll better understand the area's popularity: easily accessible parks, beaches, rocky ledges, and lighthouses, all minutes from downtown. Then head north, passing through suburban Falmouth and Yarmouth and into Freeport, home of mega–sports retailer L. L. Bean. If you look carefully during your travels through suburbia, you'll still see the vestiges of the region's heritage: sailboats and lobster boats, traps and buoys piled on lawns or along driveways and, tucked here and there, farms with farmstands brimming with fresh produce.

Greater Portland also marks a transitional point on Maine's coastline. The long sand

© TOM NANGLE

HIGHLIGHTS

◖ The Old Port: Plan to spend at least a couple of hours browsing the shops, dining, and enjoying the energy of this restored historic district (page 71).

◖ Portland Museum of Art (PMA): This museum houses works by masters such as Winslow Homer, John Marin, Andrew Wyeth, Edward Hopper, and Marsden Hartley, as well as works by Monet, Picasso, and Renoir (page 72).

◖ Victoria Mansion: This house is considered one of the most richly decorated dwellings of its period remaining in the country (page 73).

◖ Portland Observatory: Climb the 103 steps to the orb deck of the only remaining maritime signal tower on the Eastern Seaboard, and you'll be rewarded with views from the White Mountains to Casco Bay's islands (page 73).

◖ Portland Head Light: This lighthouse, commissioned by President George Washington, is fabulously sited on the rocky ledges of Cape Elizabeth (page 77).

◖ Casco Bay Tour: Take a three-hour tour on the mailboat, which stops briefly at five islands en route (page 77).

◖ Lobstering Cruise: Go out on a working lobster boat in Portland Harbor, see the sights, and perhaps return with a lobster for dinner (page 81).

◖ L. L. Bean: The empire's flagship store is in Freeport, and no trip to this shopping mecca is complete without a visit (page 96).

LOOK FOR **◖** TO FIND RECOMMENDED SIGHTS, ACTIVITIES, DINING, AND LODGING.

◖ L. L. Bean Outdoor Discovery Schools: Don't miss the opportunity for an inexpensive introduction to a new sport (page 100).

◖ Atlantic Seal Cruises: Cruise with Captain Tom Ring to Eagle Island, once home to Arctic explorer Admiral Robert Peary (page 100).

GREATER PORTLAND

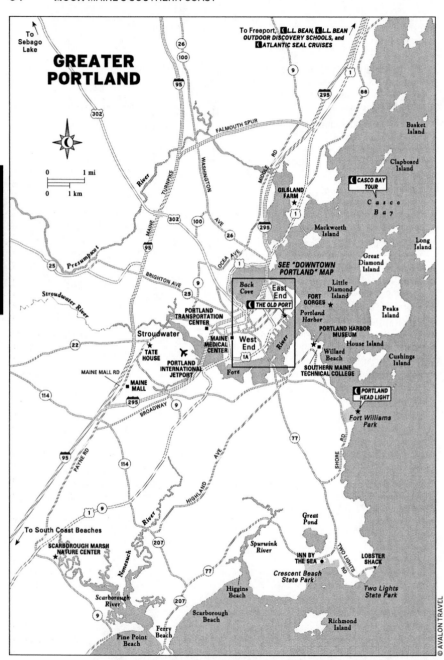

GREATER PORTLAND

To Sebago Lake

To Freeport, L.L. BEAN, L.L. BEAN OUTDOOR DISCOVERY SCHOOLS, and ATLANTIC SEAL CRUISES

0   1 mi
0   1 km

FALMOUTH SPUR

Basket Island

Clapboard Island

CASCO BAY TOUR

Casco Bay

GILSLAND FARM

Mackworth Island

Great Diamond Island

Long Island

SEE "DOWNTOWN PORTLAND" MAP

Back Cove

East End

THE OLD PORT

Little Diamond Island

FORT GORGES

Peaks Island

Portland Harbor

Stroudwater

PORTLAND TRANSPORTATION CENTER

MAINE MEDICAL CENTER

West End

Portland River

PORTLAND HARBOR MUSEUM

House Island

Cushings Island

TATE HOUSE

PORTLAND INTERNATIONAL JETPORT

Fore

Willard Beach

SOUTHERN MAINE TECHNICAL COLLEGE

MAINE MALL RD

MAINE MALL

PORTLAND HEAD LIGHT

Fort Williams Park

Stroudwater River

Presumpscot River

BRIGHTON AVE

OCEA AVE

WASHINGTON AVE

MIDDLE RD

TURNPIKE

MAINE

PAYNE RD

BROADWAY

HIGHLAND AVE

SHORE RD

TWO LIGHTS RD

To South Coast Beaches

SCARBOROUGH MARSH NATURE CENTER

Nonesuch River

Spurwink River

Great Pond

INN BY THE SEA

LOBSTER SHACK

Scarborough River

Crescent Beach State Park

Two Lights State Park

Higgins Beach

Scarborough Beach

Richmond Island

Pine Point Beach

Ferry Beach

© AVALON TRAVEL

beaches of the Southern Coast begin to give way to a different coastline, one dotted with islands and edged with a jumble of rocks and ledges interrupted by rivers and coves.

While it might seem tempting to dismiss Portland in favor of seeking the Real Maine elsewhere along the coast, the truth is, the Real Maine is here. And while Portland alone provides plenty to keep a visitor busy, it's also an excellent base for day trips to places such as the Kennebunks, Freeport, Brunswick, and Bath, where more of that Real Maine flavor awaits.

PLANNING YOUR TIME

July and August are the most popular times to visit, but Greater Portland is a year-round destination. Spring truly arrives by mid-May, when most summer outfitters begin operations at least on weekends. September is perhaps the loveliest month of the year weatherwise, and by mid-October, those fabled New England maples are turning crimson. No matter when you visit, pack layered clothing. Damp, foggy mornings can quickly give way to warm sunshine. Truly, there are usually only a handful of days each summer when folks wish they had an air conditioner, but for those days, you'll want to dress accordingly. A light sweater, fleece, or windbreaker is always handy when a sea breeze kicks up or after the sun sets.

To do the region justice, you'll want to spend at least three or four days here, more if your plans call for using Greater Portland as a base for day trips to more distant points. You can easily kill two days alone in downtown Portland, what with all the shops, museums, historical sites, waterfront, and neighborhoods to explore. If you're staying in town and are an avid walker, you won't need a car to get to the in-town must-see sights.

You will need a car to reach beyond the city. Allow a full day for a leisurely tour through South Portland and Cape Elizabeth and on to Prouts Neck in Scarborough.

Rabid shoppers should either stay in Freeport or allow at least a day for L. L. Bean's and the 100 or so outlets nearby. If you're traveling with a supershopper, don't despair. Freeport has parks and preserves that are light-years removed from the frenzy of its downtown, and from the fishing village of South Freeport, you can take an excursion boat to Eagle Island, home of Arctic explorer Admiral Peary. Really, you simply must get out on the water, whether from Portland's waterfront or from South Freeport. Hop a ferry to one of the islands of Casco Bay, take an evening sail, an excursion to Eagle Island, or even a paddle around the islands in a kayak.

HISTORY

Portland's downtown, a crooked-finger peninsula projecting into Casco Bay and today defined vaguely by I-295 at its "knuckle," was named Machigonne (Great Neck) by the Wabanaki, the Native Americans who held sway when English settlers first arrived in 1632. Characteristically, the Brits renamed the region Falmouth (it included present-day Falmouth, Portland, South Portland, Westbrook, and Cape Elizabeth) and the peninsula Falmouth Neck, but it was 130 years before they secured real control of the area. Anglo-French squabbles, spurred by the governments' conflicts in Europe, drew in the Wabanaki from Massachusetts to Nova Scotia. Falmouth was only one of the battlegrounds, and it was a fairly minor one. Relative calm resumed in the 1760s, only to be broken by the stirrings of rebellion centered on Boston. When Falmouth's citizens expressed support for the incipient revolution, the punishment was a 1775 naval onslaught that wiped out 75 percent of the houses—a debacle that created a decade-long setback. In 1786, Falmouth Neck became Portland, a thriving trading community where shipping flourished until the 1807 imposition of the Embargo Act. Severing trade and effectively shutting down Portland Harbor for a year and a half, the legislation did more harm to America's fledgling colonies than to the French and British it was designed to punish.

In 1820, when Maine became a state, Portland was named its capital. The city became a crucial transportation hub with the arrival of the railroad. The Civil War was barely a blip in

Portland's history, but the year after it ended, the city suffered a devastating blow: exuberant Fourth of July festivities in 1866 sparked a conflagration that virtually leveled the city. The Great Fire spared only the Portland Observatory and a chunk of the West End. Evidence of the city's Victorian rebirth remains today in many downtown neighborhoods.

After World War II, Portland slipped into decline for several years, but that is over. The city's waterfront revival began in the 1970s and continues today, despite commercial competition from South Portland's Maine Mall; Congress Street has blossomed as an arts and retail district; public green space is increasing; and an influx of immigrants is changing the city's cultural makeup. With the new century, Portland is on a roll.

Portland

Often compared to San Francisco (an oft-cited, unchallenged, but never verified statistic boasts it has more restaurants per capita than any city but San Francisco), Portland is small, friendly, and easily explored on foot—although at times, it may seem that no matter which direction you head, it's uphill. The heart of Portland is the peninsula jutting into Casco Bay. It's bordered by the Eastern and Western Promenades, Back Cove, and the working waterfront. Salty sea breezes cool summer days and make winter ones seen even chillier. Unlike that other city by the bay, snow frequently blankets Portland from December into March.

Portland is Maine's most ethnically diverse city, with active refugee resettlement programs and dozens of languages spoken in the schools. Although salty sailors can still be found along the waterfront, Portland is increasingly a professional community, with young, upwardly mobile residents spiffing up Victorian houses and infusing new energy and money into the city's neighborhoods.

The region's cultural hub, Portland has a striking art museum housing three centuries of art and architecture and a world-class permanent collection, performing arts centers, active historical and preservation groups, an art school and a university, a symphony orchestra, numerous galleries, coffeehouses, and enough activities to keep culture vultures busy well into the night, especially in the thriving, handsomely restored Old Port and the up-and-coming Arts District.

Portland's also a sports- and outdoor-lovers' playground, with trails for running, biking, skating, and cross-country skiing, watersports aplenty, and a beloved minor league baseball team, the Sea Dogs. When city folks desire to escape, they often hop a ferry for one of the islands of Casco Bay or head to one of the parks, preserves, or beaches in the suburbs.

Still, Portland remains a major seaport. Lobster boats, commercial fishing vessels, long-distance passenger boats, cruise ships, and local ferries dominate the working waterfront, and the briny scent of the sea—or bait—seasons the air.

PORTLAND NEIGHBORHOODS

The best way to appreciate the character of Portland's neighborhoods is on foot. So much of Portland can (and should) be covered on foot that it would take a book to list all the possibilities, but several dedicated volunteer groups have produced guides to facilitate the process.

Greater Portland Landmarks (207/774-5561, www.portlandlandmarks.org) is the doyenne, founded in 1964 to preserve Portland's historic architecture and promote responsible construction. The organization has published more than a dozen books and booklets, including *Discover Historic Portland on Foot,* a packet of four well-researched walking-tour guides to architecturally historic sections of Portland's peninsula: Old Port, Western Promenade, State Street, and Congress Street. It's available for $5.95 at local

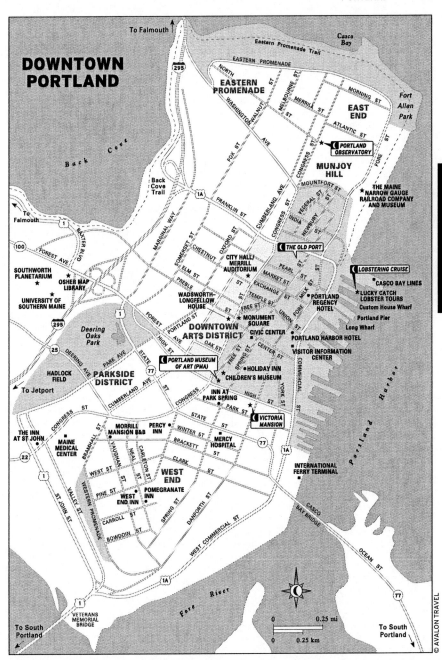

DOWNTOWN PORTLAND

To Falmouth

Casco Bay

Eastern Promenade Trail

EASTERN PROMENADE

EASTERN PROMENADE

NORTH ST

MELBOURNE ST

WASHINGTON/WALNUT ST

MERRILL ST

MORNING ST

EAST END

Fort Allen Park

ATLANTIC ST

CONGRESS ST

FORE ST

★ PORTLAND OBSERVATORY

MUNJOY HILL

THE MAINE NARROW GAUGE RAILROAD COMPANY AND MUSEUM

MOUNTFORT ST

FEDERAL ST

INDIA ST

NEWBURY ST

FOX ST

FRANKLIN ST

CUMBERLAND AVE

CONGRESS ST

THE OLD PORT

Back Cove

Back Cove Trail

To Falmouth

FOREST AVE

BAXTER BLVD

MARGINAL WAY

SOMERSET ST

CHESTNUT

OXFORD ST

ELM ST

PREBLE

SOUTHWORTH PLANETARIUM ★

OSHER MAP LIBRARY ★

UNIVERSITY OF SOUTHERN MAINE ★

CITY HALL/ MERRILL AUDITORIUM

MARKET ST

PEARL ST

EXCHANGE ST

TEMPLE ST

MLK

FORE ST

UNION ST

LOBSTERING CRUISE

CASCO BAY LINES

★ LUCKY CATCH LOBSTER TOURS

Custom House Wharf

Portland Pier

Long Wharf

WADSWORTH-LONGFELLOW HOUSE

FREE ST

PORTLAND REGENCY HOTEL

Deering Oaks Park

PORTLAND AVE

HIGH ST

FOREST AVE

DOWNTOWN ARTS DISTRICT

MONUMENT SQUARE

CIVIC CENTER

PORTLAND HARBOR HOTEL

VISITOR INFORMATION CENTER

OAK ST

PARK AVE

STATE ST

77

PARKSIDE DISTRICT

PORTLAND MUSEUM OF ART (PMA) ★

SPRING ST

CENTER ST

COMMERCIAL ST

HADLOCK FIELD

HOLIDAY INN

CHILDREN'S MUSEUM

YORK ST

Portland Harbor

To Jetport

CUMBERLAND AVE

CONGRESS ST

INN AT PARK SPRING

STATE ST

PARK ST

HIGH ST

VICTORIA MANSION ★

THE INN AT ST JOHN

MAINE MEDICAL CENTER

BRAMHALL ST

VAUGHAN ST

MORRILL MANSION B&B

PERCY INN

NEAL ST

CARLETON ST

WINTER ST

BRACKETT

MERCY HOSPITAL

WEST END

CLARK ST

INTERNATIONAL FERRY TERMINAL

WEST ST

WESTERN PROMENADE

VALLEY ST

PINE ST

WEST END INN

POMEGRANATE INN

SPRING ST

DAMFORTH ST

WEST COMMERCIAL ST

CASCO BAY BRIDGE

OCEAN ST

CARROLL ST

BOWDOIN ST

Fore River

To South Portland

VETERANS MEMORIAL BRIDGE

To South Portland

0   0.25 mi

0   0.25 km

GREATER PORTLAND

CASCO BAY ISLANDS

Casco Bay is dotted with so many islands that an early explorer thought there must be at least one for every day of the year and so dubbed them the Calendar Islands. Truthfully, there aren't quite that many, even if you count all the ledges that appear at low tide. No matter, the islands are as much a part of Portland life as the Old Port.

Casco Bay Lines is the islands' lifeline, providing car and passenger service daily in summer. Perhaps the best way to see the highlights is aboard the daily mail-boat run. Indeed, on hot days, it may seem as if half the city's population is hopping a ferry to enjoy the cool breezes and calming views.

PEAKS ISLAND

Peaks Island is a mere 20-minute ferry ride from downtown Portland, so it's no surprise that it has the largest year-round population. Historically a popular vacation spot – two lodges were built for Civil War veterans – it's now an increasingly popular suburb.

Although you can walk the island's perimeter in 3-4 hours, the best way to see it is to take a bike ($5 extra on the ferry) and pedal around clockwise. It can take less than an hour to do the five-mile island circuit, but plan on relaxing on the beach, savoring the views, and visiting the museums. Rental bikes are available on the island from Brad Burkholder at **Brad's and Wyatt's Bike Shop** (115 Island Ave., Peaks Island, 207/766-5631, about $20/day, hourly rental available, 10 A.M.-6 P.M.).

Another way to see the island is on a golf-cart tour with **Island Tours** (207/653-2549, islandtours@att.net, $15 adults, $12 seniors, $8 child), which offers a variety of 90-minute island tours as well as one-hour sunset tours ($10 adults, $8 seniors, $5 child). Admission to the Fifth Maine Regiment Museum is included in longer tours.

Civil War buffs have two museums worth a visit. The **Fifth Maine Regiment Center** (45 Seashore Ave., Peaks Island, 207/766-3330, www.fifthmainemuseum.org, 11 A.M.-4 P.M. daily July 1-Labor Day, to 5 P.M. weekends late May-July 1 and early Sept.-mid-Oct., $5 donation requested), a Queen Anne-style cottage built by Civil War veterans in 1888, now houses exhibits on the war and island history. Just a few steps away is the **Eighth Maine Regimental Memorial** (13 Eighth Maine Ave., Peaks Island, 207/766-5086, noon-3 P.M. Tues.-Sat. July 1-early Sept., $5 donation requested). Tours detail the building's fascinating history and its collection of artifacts pertaining to the Eighth Maine as well as material on the island, World War II, and more. Rustic lodging is available.

Another museum perhaps worthy of a visit just for its quirkiness is the **Umbrella Cover Museum** (207/766-4496), where owner Nancy 3. Hoffman (yes, 3) displays her collection.

Hungry? **The Cockeyed Gull** (78 Island Ave., 207/766-2880, www.cockeyedgull.com) is the best choice for either lunch or dinner.

GREAT DIAMOND ISLAND

Great Diamond is a totally different scene. In 1891, the U.S. government began building an Army post on Great Diamond, a quick ferryboat ride from the Portland harbor front. Completed in 1907, **Fort McKinley** (named after President William McKinley) became part of Portland Harbor's five-fort defense system during World Wars I and II. When peace descended, the fort's red-brick structures were left to crumble for nearly five decades. In 1984, developers stepped in, bought the derelicts, and began restoration – albeit not without financial setbacks and opposition from environmental organizations.

Today, the 193-acre **Diamond Cove** enclave boasts barracks-turned-townhomes, single-family houses, a general store (open daily late May-Labor Day), outdoor theater, a beach bar (open mid-June-mid-September), an art gallery, no cars (only bikes and golf carts), and the **Diamond's Edge Restaurant** (207/766-5850, www.diamondsedge.com).

GREAT CHEBEAGUE

Everyone calls Great Chebeague just "Chebeague" (shuh-BIG). Yes, there's a Little Che-

© HILARY NANGLE

PEAKS ISLAND

The Casco Bay Lines ferry dock on Peaks Island requires precise maneuvering by the captain.

beague, but it's a state-owned park, and no one lives there. Chebeague is the largest of the bay's islands – 4.5 miles long, 1.5 miles wide – and the relatively level terrain makes it easy to get around. Don't plan to bring a car; it's too complicated to arrange.

You can bike the leisurely 10-mile circuit of the island in a couple of hours, but unless you're in a hurry, allow time to relax and enjoy your visit. Pick up an island map at the Portland terminal or on the ferry; all the high points are listed, including two beach access points off North Road.

If the tide is right, cross the sandspit from The Hook and explore **Little Chebeague.** Start out about two hours before low tide (preferably around new moon or full moon, when the most water drains away) and plan to be back on Chebeague no later than two hours after low tide.

Back on Great Chebeague, when you're ready for a swim, head for **Hamilton Beach,** a

beautiful small stretch of sand lined with dune grass, not far from the Chebeague Island Inn. Also on this part of the island is **East End Point,** with a spectacular panoramic view of Halfway Rock and the bay.

Chebeague Transportation Company, from Cousins Island, Yarmouth, also services the island.

EAGLE ISLAND

Seventeen-acre Eagle Island (207/624-6080, www.pearyeagleisland.org, 10 A.M.-5 P.M. mid-June-early Sept.) juts out of Casco Bay, rising to a rocky promontory 40 feet above the crashing surf. On the bluff's crest, Robert Edwin Peary, the first man to lead a party of fellow men to the North Pole without the use of mechanical or electrical devices, built his dream home. It's now a state historic site that's accessible via excursion boats from Portland or Freeport. The half-day trip usually includes a narrated cruise to the island and time to tour the house, filled with Peary family artifacts, and wander the nature trails. (Note: Trails are usually closed until approximately mid-July to protect nesting eider ducks).

Peary envisioned the island's rocky bluff as a ship's prow and built his house to resemble a pilot house. Wherever possible, he used indigenous materials from the island in the construction, including timber drift, fallen trees, beach rocks, and cement mixed with screened beach sand and small pebbles. From the library, Peary corresponded with world leaders, adventurers, and explorers, such as Teddy Roosevelt, the Wright Brothers, Roald Amundsen, and Ernest Shackleton, and planned his expeditions. Peary reached the North Pole on April 6, 1909, and his wife, Josephine, was on Eagle when she received word via telegraph of her husband's accomplishment. After Peary's death, in 1920, the family continued to spend summers on Eagle until Josephine's death, in 1955. It was a unanimous family decision to donate the island to the state of Maine. Check the website for information on guided tours to the island led by Peary's grandson.

GREATER PORTLAND

GREATER PORTLAND

LIGHTHOUSES AND PARKS TOUR

Whether in a car or on a bike, it's easy to loop through South Portland and Cape Elizabeth on a route that takes in lighthouses, forts, beaches, and parks.

Begin just over the Casco Bay Bridge from downtown Portland (Rte. 77), take Broadway and continue to the end at **Southern Maine Community College (SMCC)**, overlooking the bay. (Best time to come here is evenings and weekends, when there's ample parking.) Unless it's foggy (when the signal is deafening) or thundering (when you'll expose yourself to lightning), walk out along the 1,000-foot granite breakwater to the **Spring Point Ledge Light,** with fabulous views in every direction. Also here are picnic benches, the remains of Fort Preble, and the Portland Harbor Museum. At the southern edge of the SMCC campus is the **Spring Point Shoreline Walkway,** a scenic three-mile pathway with views off to House, Peaks, and Cushings Islands. At the end of the shoreway, you'll reach crescent-shaped **Willard Beach,** a neighborhoody sort of place with lifeguards, a changing building, a snack bar, and those same marvelous views.

From the SMCC campus, return on Broadway to the major intersection with Cottage Road and bear left. Cottage Road becomes Shore Road at the Cape Elizabeth town line. Loop into Fort Williams Park and make a pilgrimage to **Portland Head Light** before continuing on Shore Road to its intersection with Route 77. Bear left and follow to Two Lights Road and follow signs to 40-acre **Two Lights State Park.** Almost a vest-pocket park, it has picnicking and restroom facilities, but its biggest asset is the panoramic ocean view from atop a onetime gun battery. Summer admission is $4.50 adults 12-64, $1 kids 5-11.

Before or after visiting the park, take a left just before the park entrance (it's a continuation of Two Lights Road; the sign says Lighthouses). Continue to the parking lot at the end, where you'll see the signal towers for which Two Lights is named. (There's no access to either one; only one still works.) If you haven't brought a picnic for the state park, enjoy the food and the view at **The Lobster Shack.**

To eke out some beach time, return to Route 77 and continue to **Crescent Beach State Park,** a 243-acre park with changing rooms, lifeguard, restrooms, picnic tables, and a snack bar. Admission is $3.50 adults, 12-64, $1 kids 5-11. Directly offshore is Saco Bay's **Richmond Island,** a 200-acre private preserve with a checkered past dating to the 17th century.

---

bookstores, some gift shops, and the Visitor Information Center (245 Commercial St., 207/772-5800).

Also available at the Visitor Information Center is a map, $1, detailing 36 significant **antislavery sites** in Portland. It also includes stories and information about the slave trade and what life was like for blacks during the slavery era. Six significant sites, each marked, are included in a 1.6-mile walking tour.

The *Portland Women's History Trail* details four loops—Congress Street, Munjoy Hill, State Street, and the West End—with about 20 stops on each loop. Among the sites: a long-gone chewing-gum factory where teenage girls worked 10-hour shifts. The trail guide is available for $8.50 in selected bookstores and at the Maine History Gallery gift shop (489 Congress St., Portland, 207/879-0427).

Portland Trails (1 India St., Portland, 207/775-2411, www.trails.org), a dynamic membership conservation organization incorporated in 1991, continually adds to the mileage it has mapped out for hiking and biking around Portland. The group's accomplishments include the 2.1-mile Eastern Promenade Trail, a landscaped bayfront dual pathway circling the base of Munjoy Hill and linking East End Beach to the Old Port, and a continuing trail connecting the Eastern Prom with the 3.5-mile Back Cove Trail, on the other side of I-295. Nearly two dozen trails are maintained, and the group also holds organized events—a great way to

WINSLOW HOMER

Discovering Maine in his early 40s, Winslow Homer (1836-1910) was smitten – enough to spend the last 27 years of his life in Prouts Neck (Scarborough, south of Portland), a small fishing village gradually morphing into an exclusive summer enclave. Here, in a cluttered, rustic studio converted from a onetime stable (recently acquired by the Portland Museum of Art, which eventually plans to open it to the public on a limited basis), he produced his finest works, the seascapes that have become so familiar to us all. He painted the sea in every mood, the rocks in every light, the snow in all its bleakness, the hardy trees bent to the wind. Occasional forays to the Bahamas, the Adirondacks, and the Canadian wilderness inspired other themes, but Prouts Neck always lured him back. Homer's last work, an oil titled *Driftwood*, painted in 1909 when his health was in major decline, depicts once again the struggle of man against the roiling surf that Homer knew so intimately from his life on the coast of Maine.

everyone hopping until after midnight. Police keep a close eye on the district, but it can get a bit dicey after 11 P.M. on weekends. Caveat emptor—or maybe caveat peregrinator!

At 10:30 A.M. daily July–September, knowledgeable guides from Greater Portland Landmarks (207/774-5561, www.portlandlandmarks.org) lead fascinating 90-minute **Old Port walking tours** in downtown Portland. No reservations needed. Buy tickets at the Visitor Information Center (245 Commercial St.), where the tours begin and end. Cost is $8 pp; kids under 16 with an adult are free.

Congress Street/Downtown Arts District

Bit by bit, once-declining Congress Street is becoming revitalized, showcasing the best of the city's culture. Artists, starving and otherwise, spend much of their time here, thanks largely to encouragement from the energetic grassroots Downtown Arts District Association (DADA). Galleries, artists' studios, coffeehouses, cafés and bistros, craft shops, two libraries, the State Theatre, the Merrill Auditorium (in City Hall), the Portland Museum of Art, the Maine College of Art, and even L. L. Bean and the Portland Public Market are all part of the ongoing renaissance.

West End

Probably the most diverse of the city's downtown neighborhoods, and one that largely escaped the Great Fire of 1866, the West End includes the historically and architecturally splendid Western Promenade, Maine Medical Center (the state's largest hospital), the city's best B&Bs, a gay-friendly community with a laissez-faire attitude, a host of cafés and restaurants, as well as a few niches harboring the homeless and forlorn.

Munjoy Hill/East End

A once slightly down-at-the-heels neighborhood enclave with a pull-'em-up-by-the-bootstraps attitude, Portland's East End is rapidly gentrifying. Munjoy Hill is probably best

meet some locals. Contact Portland Trails for a colorful foldout map of Portland's entire trail and park system—including some proposed routes—a joint effort of Portland Trails and the Greater Portland Council of Governments' Kids and Transportation Program. Better still, join Portland Trails ($35 a year) and support its ambitious efforts.

◖ The Old Port

Tony shops, cobblestone sidewalks, replica streetlights, and a casual, upmarket crowd (most of the time) set the scene for a district once filled with derelict buildings. The 1970s revival of the Old Port has infused funds, foot traffic, and flair into this part of town. Scores of unusual shops, ethnic restaurants, and spontaneous street-corner music make it a fun area to visit year-round. Nightlife centers on the Old Port, where a couple of dozen bars keep

GREATER PORTLAND

Portland's waterfront wharves are lined with both pleasure and working craft.

known for the distinctive wooden tower that adorns its summit.

Named for George Munjoy, a wealthy 17th-century resident, this district has a host of architectural and historic landmarks—well worth a walking tour. Fortunately, Greater Portland Landmarks (207/774-5561, www.portlandlandmarks.org) has produced a 24-page booklet, *Munjoy Hill Historic Guide* ($3), which documents more than 60 notable sites, including the National Historic Register Eastern Cemetery and, with spectacular harbor views, the Eastern Promenade and Fort Allen Park. From early June to early October, Landmarks also offers guided walking tours of the historic **Eastern Cemetery,** the oldest burial ground on the peninsula, at 10:30 A.M. on Thursdays, beginning at the Portland Observatory (138 Congress St.). Cost is $7 adult, free under 16.

Bayside and Parkside
A Babel of languages reverberates in these districts just below Portland City Hall. Bayside experienced the arrival of refugees—Cambodian, Laotian, Vietnamese, Central European, and Afghan families—from war-torn lands during the 1980s and 1990s. Nowadays, you'll hear references to Somali Town, an area named for all the resettled refugees from that shattered country. Others have come from Sudan and Ethiopia. Portland's active Refugee Resettlement Program has assisted all. Many have found employment with Barber Foods, a fantastically conscientious firm that hires many new immigrants in its processing plant and provides opportunities for employees to learn English and obtain social services. Many newcomers have also become entrepreneurs, opening restaurants and small markets catering to their compatriots but increasingly gaining customers among local residents. Real-estate pressures are contributing to changes in these neighborhoods, too. The city is working to relocate scrap-metal yards and replace them with housing and small businesses.

Beyond the Peninsula
At the western edge of Portland, close to the Portland Jetport, is the historic area known as **Stroudwater,** once an essential link in Maine water transport. The 20-mile-long **Cumberland and Oxford Canal,** handdug in 1828, ran through here as part of the timber-shipping route linking Portland Harbor, the Fore and Presumpscot Rivers, and Sebago Lake. Twenty-eight wooden locks allowed vessels to rise the 265 feet between sea level and the lake. By 1870, trains took over the route, condemning the canal to oblivion. Centerpiece of the Stroudwater area today is the historic 18th-century Tate House.

SIGHTS
◖ Portland Museum of Art (PMA)
Three centuries of art and architecture: That's what you'll discover at Maine's oldest (since 1882) and finest art museum, the Portland Museum of Art (7 Congress Sq., Portland,

207/775-6148, recorded info 207/773-2787 or 800/639-4067, www.portlandmuseum.org, 10 A.M.–5 P.M., to 9 P.M. Fri., closed Mon. mid-Oct.–late May, $10 adults, $8 seniors and students, $4 ages 6–17, free admission 5–9 P.M. every Friday). The museum's topflight collection of American and impressionist masters and fine and decorative arts is displayed in three architecturally stunning, connected buildings: the award-winning Charles Shipman Payson building, designed by I. M. Pei and opened in 1983, the newly restored Federal-era McLellan House, and the beaux-arts L. D. M. Sweat Memorial Galleries, designed by noted Maine architect John Calvin Stevens. The museum also has a well-stocked gift shop and a pleasant café that's open for lunch daily (11 A.M.–4 P.M.) and for dinner Friday (to 7:30 P.M.). Call for information about family activities, lectures, and other events.

◖ Victoria Mansion

Jaws literally drop when their owners enter the Italianate Victoria Mansion, also called the Morse-Libby Mansion (109 Danforth St., Portland, 207/772-4841, www.victoria-mansion.org, 10 A.M.–4 P.M. Mon.–Sat. and 1–5 P.M. Sun. May–Oct., special hours in Dec., $10 adults, $9 seniors, $3 6–17, holiday season $12 adults, $5 ages 6–17, $25 per family), widely considered the most magnificently ornamented dwelling of its period remaining in the country. The national Historic Landmark is rife with Victoriana—carved marble fireplaces, elaborate porcelain and paneling, a free-standing mahogany staircase, gilded glass chandeliers, a recently restored 6- by 25-foot stained-glass ceiling window, and unbelievable trompe l'oeil touches. It's even more spectacular at Christmas, with yards of roping, festooned trees, and carolers. (This is the best time to bring kids, as the house itself may not particularly intrigue them.) The mansion was built in the late 1850s by Ruggles Sylvester Morse, a Maine-born entrepreneur whose New Orleans–based fortune enabled him to hire 93 craftsmen to complete the house. The interior, designed

The Victoria Mansion is a nationally renowned gem, although you wouldn't know it from the exterior.

by Gustave Herter, still boasts 90 percent of the original furnishings. Guided 45-minute tours begin every half hour (on the quarter hour) in season; tours are self-guided during the holidays.

◖ Portland Observatory

Providing a head-swiveling view of Portland (and the White Mountains on a clear day), the octagonal red-painted Portland Observatory (138 Congress St., Portland, 207/774-5561, www.portlandlandmarks.org, 10 A.M.–5 P.M. late May–Columbus Day, last tour at 4:30 P.M., $6 adults, $4 ages 6–16) is the only remaining marine signal tower on the Eastern Seaboard. Built in 1807 at a cost of $5,000 by Captain Lemuel Moody to keep track of the port's shipping activity, the tower has 122 tons of rock ballast in its base. Admission in those days (only men were allowed to climb the 103 interior steps) was 12.5 cents. Today, admission includes

© TOM NANGLE

Climb the 103 steps to the orb deck of the Portland Observatory for 360-degree views.

the small museum at the tower's base and a guided tour to the top.

The Longfellow Connection

A few blocks down Congress Street from the PMA, you'll step back in time to the era of Portland-born poet Henry Wadsworth Longfellow, who lived in the accurately restored **Wadsworth-Longfellow House** (485 Congress St., Portland, 207/774-1822, www.mainehistory.org, 10 A.M.–4 P.M. Mon.–Sat., noon–4 P.M. Sun. May 1–Oct. 31, special holiday hours Nov. and Dec., $7 adults, $6 seniors and students, $3 ages 5–17), as a child in the early 1800s—long before the brick mansion was dwarfed by surrounding high-rises. Wadsworth and Longfellow family furnishings fill the three-story house (owned by the Maine Historical Society), and savvy guides provide insight into Portland's 19th-century life. Don't miss the urban oasis—a wonderfully peaceful garden—behind

the house (same hours, free admission). Buy tickets at the adjacent Center for Maine History, which also houses the **Maine History Gallery** (489 Congress St., 207/774-1822, www.mainehistory.org, 10 A.M.–5 P.M. Mon.–Sat., noon–5 P.M. Sun., $4 adults, $3 seniors, $2 children), where you can take in the Maine Historical Society's current exhibits and find an extensive collection of Maine history books in the gift shop.

Maine Narrow Gauge Railroad and Museum

A three-mile ride along Portland's waterfront is the highlight of a visit to the Maine Narrow Gauge Railroad Company and Museum (58 Fore St., Portland, 207/828-0814, www.mngrr.org). The museum (10 A.M.–4 P.M. daily late May–late Oct., weekends only off-season, $2 adult, $1 seniors and ages 3–12 or free with train ticket) owns more than three dozen train cars and has others on long-term loan—most from Maine's five historic narrow-gauge railroads (the last one closed in 1943). You can board a number of the cars and see others undergoing restoration. For a fee, you can ride the two-foot rails aboard a multicar train. The schedule roughly follows museum hours, with rides on the hour ($10 adults, $9 seniors, $6 ages 3–12). The track edges Casco Bay along the Eastern Promenade—a short but enjoyable excursion that's a real kid pleaser. Years ago, hundreds of steam engines were built here, but steam locomotives now operate only for special occasions. Trains also operate during school vacation weeks; call for schedule. At the eastern end of Fore Street, turn at the railroad-crossing sign on the waterside; the museum is at the back of the complex.

Museum of African Culture

Founded in 1998, the Museum of African Culture (13 Brown St., Portland, 207/871-7188, www.museumafricanculture. org, 10:30 A.M.–4 P.M. Tues.–Sat., $5 donation) is the brainchild of Nigerian-born Oscar Mokeme (the director) and Arthur

© TOM NANGLE

Kids love riding the Narrow Gauge Railroad along the Eastern Prom waterfront.

Aleshire. It's devoted to sub-Saharan African arts and culture. Among the museum's 300 or so treasures—not all on display at once—are Nigerian tribal masks and Benin lost-wax bronzes. The museum also has an ambitious outreach program, educating the community about African art and culture. Ask about Friday night programs.

Children's Museum of Maine

Here's the answer to parents' prayers—a whole museum in downtown Portland catering to kids. At the Children's Museum of Maine (P.O. Box 4041, 142 Free St., next to the Portland Museum of Art, Portland 04101, 207/828-1234, www.kitetails.com, 10 A.M.–5 P.M. Mon.–Sat., noon to 5 P.M. Sun., closed Mon. early Sept.–late May, $7, children 1 and younger free, free admission 5–8 P.M. first Fri. of each month), lots of hands-on displays encourage interaction and guarantee involvement for a couple of hours. What's here? A submarine, computer lab, TV studio, L. L. Bean's Discovery Woods, a space shuttle, a supermarket, bank (with an ATM), lobster boat, a camera obscura (one of only three in the country, $3 for that exhibit only) and more than a dozen other activities. There's even an animal hospital. Call to check on the special-events schedule.

Portland Freedom Trail

Pick up a copy of this free map and brochure detailing a self-guided walking tour of a baker's dozen marked sights related to Portland's role in Maine's Underground Railway (www.portlandfreedomtrail.org). Among the highlights are the Abyssinian Meeting House, the third-oldest African American Meeting House still standing in the United States (undergoing restoration); First Parish Unitarian Universalist Church, where abolitionist William Lloyd Garrison spoke in 1832; Mariners' Church, location of an antislavery bookstore and print shop that printed the first Afrocentric history of the world; and Franklin Street Wharf, where stowaway slaves often arrived on vessels from Southern ports.

Breweries

Look for the keg topping the flagpole at **Shipyard Brewery** (86 Newbury St., Portland, 207/761-0807, www.shipyard.com). Tours of the award-winning microbrewery are offered on the hour noon–4 P.M. Tours begin with a short promotional video explaining the brewing process and end with a tasting. Even if you're not a beer/ale drinker, go and enjoy the root beer that's also brewed on the premises.

Other Portland breweries offering tours are **Allagash Brewing Company** (50 Industrial Way, 207/878-5385), at 3 P.M. weekdays; **Beary's Brewing Company** (38 Evergreen Dr., 207/878-2337), at 2:30 P.M. weekdays; and **Casco Bay Brewing Company** (57 Industrial Way, 207/797-2020), by appointment.

BEYOND THE DOWNTOWN PENINSULA
Seeing Stars

Under a 30-foot dome with comfy theater seats and a state-of-the-art laser system, the **Southworth Planetarium** (96 Falmouth St., Science Building, lower level, University of Southern Maine, Portland, 207/780-4249, www.usm.maine.edu/~planet, 7 and 8:30 P.M. Fri. and Sat., $5–6 adults, $4–6 seniors and children) presents astronomy shows. Computer-savvy kids will head for the interactive computers in the exhibit area; the gift shop stocks astronaut ice cream and other science-type stuff. For recorded information on moon and planet positions, eclipses, and other astronomical happenings, call the **Skywatch Hotline** (207/780-4719). Take Exit 6B off I-295 and go west on Forest Avenue to Falmouth Street (left turn). The Science Building is on the left, after the parking lot.

Osher Map Library

Also on the University of Southern Maine's campus is the Osher Map Library (207/780-4850 or 800/800-4876, ext. 4850, www.usm.maine. edu/~maps, call for schedule). The library's collection, primarily a teaching resource, documents the history of Western cartography from its inception to modern times. Themed exhib-

its feature highlights from the library's original maps, atlases, geographies, and globes dating from the late 15th century. Other artifacts include texts depicting explorers' narratives, accounts of early travelers, and works of cosmography, astronomy, navigation, and geography.

Tate House

Just down the street from the Portland International Jetport, in the Stroudwater district, is the 1755 Tate House (1270 Westbrook St., 207/774-6177, www.tatehouse. org, 10 A.M.–4 P.M. Tues.–Sat. 1–4 P.M. and first Sun. of each month June 15–Oct. 15, $7 adults, $5 seniors, $2 age 6–12), a National Historic Landmark owned by the Colonial Dames of America. Built by Captain George Tate, who was prominent in shipbuilding, the house has superb period furnishings and a lovely 18th-century herb garden (more than 70 varieties) overlooking the Stroudwater River. Tours last 40 minutes. Wednesdays mid-June–mid-September are "summer garden days," when tea and goodies follow tours of the garden (for an extra charge). Other special hour-long tours focusing on the architecture and the historic Stroudwater neighborhood can be arranged by appointment. Across the street, in the Means House, is the museum's gift shop. From downtown Portland, it's 3.2 miles; take Congress Street West (Rte. 22), under I-295, and out as far as Waldo Street, just after the Fore River. Turn left onto Waldo and then turn right onto Westbrook Street. If you find yourself with spare time at the Portland Jetport, Tate House is an easy walk from the terminal. Ask for directions at the airport information desk.

Portland Harbor Museum

The maritime history of Casco Bay and Maine is the focus of the small Portland Harbor Museum (Fort Rd., South Portland, 207/799-6337, www.PortlandHarborMuseum.org, 10 A.M.–4:30 P.M. daily late May–mid-Oct., and Fri.–Sun. spring and fall, $4 adults) on the waterfront campus of Southern Maine Community College (SMCC). To reach the museum, head over from downtown Portland (Rte. 77) and continue onto Broadway. Watch for SMCC signs. The museum now holds the title to the nearby Spring Point Ledge lighthouse, which is open for tours periodically during the summer. Call for the schedule. Also nearby are the remains of Fort Preble and the Spring Point Shoreline Walkway leading to Willard Beach.

◖ Portland Head Light

Just four miles from downtown Portland, Fort Williams, in Cape Elizabeth, feels a world away. This oceanfront town park, a former military base, is home to Portland Head Light (1000 Shore Rd., Fort Williams Park, Cape Elizabeth, 207/799-2661, www.portland-headlight.com, open dawn–dusk). Commissioned by President George Washington and first lighted in 1791, it has been immortalized in poetry, photography, and philately. The surf here is awesome—perhaps too awesome. The *Annie C. Maguire* was ship-

Portland Head Light guards the ledgy shores of Cape Elizabeth.

© HILARY NANGLE

wrecked below the lighthouse on Christmas Eve, 1886. There's no access to the 58-foot automated light tower, but the superbly restored keeper's house has become **The Museum at Portland Head Light** (10 A.M.–4 P.M. daily late May–mid-Oct. and weekends late spring and late fall, but call first to confirm, $2 adults, $1 kids 6–18). It's filled with local history and lighthouse memorabilia. The 90-acre oceanfront park offers much else to explore, including ruins of the fort and the Goddard mansion. Walk the trails, play a game of tennis, dip your toes in the surf at the rocky beach, but be careful, as there's a strong undertow here. You might even catch the Portland Symphony Orchestra, which occasionally performs here in summer. The grassy headlands are great places to watch the boat traffic going in and out of Portland Harbor. Bring a picnic lunch, and don't forget a kite. From downtown Portland, take Route 77 and then Broadway, Cottage Road, and Shore Road.

TOURS
◖ Casco Bay Tour

Casco Bay Lines (Commercial and Franklin Sts., Old Port, Portland, 207/774-7871, www.cascobaylines.com), the nation's oldest continuously operating ferry system (since the 1920s), is the lifeline between Portland and six inhabited Casco Bay islands. What better way to sample the islands than to go along for the three-hour ride with mail, groceries, and island residents? The Casco Bay Lines mail boat stops—briefly—at **Long Island, Chebeague, Cliff,** and **Little** and **Great Diamond Islands.** Departures are 10 A.M. and 2:15 P.M. daily mid-June–Labor Day (plus 7:45 A.M. weekdays), 10 A.M. and 2:45 P.M. other months. Fares are $13 adults, $11.50 seniors, and $6.50 ages 5–9. The longest cruise on the Casco Bay Lines schedule is the five-hour, 45-minute narrated summertime trip (late June–Labor Day) to **Bailey Island,** with a two-hour stopover, departing from Portland at 10 A.M. daily ($18.50 adults, $16.50 seniors, $8.50 ages 5–9). Dogs (on leashes) and bicycles need separate tickets—$6 for bikes, $3.75 for animals.

Walking Tours

The best tours of the area are offered by **Greater Portland Landmarks** (207/774-5561, www.portlandlandmarks.org), which sponsors neighborhood walking tours as well as an annual **summer tour program,** featuring four or five walking trips and excursions to offshore islands, historic churches, revamped buildings, and gardens. Many of the destinations are private or otherwise inaccessible, so these are special opportunities. Registration is limited, and there's only one trip to each site. Tours run mid-July–mid-October, primarily on weekends.

Land and Sea Tours

Three commercial operators offer area land-and-sea tours, but frankly, none is first rate. On each, guides often present incorrect information. Still, such tours are a good way to get the city's general layout. The best of the lot is the 1.5-hour narrated sightseeing tour of Portland in a trolley-bus by **Mainely Tours** (3 Moulton St., Old Port, Portland, 207/774-0808, www.mainelytours.com). Cost is $16 adults, $15 seniors, $9 ages 3–12. You can combine this tour with a 90-minute Lighthouse Lover's boat tour on Casco Bay. The combined price is $27 adult, $25 senior, and $16 kids.

An alternative, especially if you're traveling with kids, is the 60–70 minute **Downeast Duck Adventures** (office at Harbor View Gifts, 177 Commercial St., 207/774-3825, www.downeastducktours.com, early June–early Oct., $22 adult, $19 senior, $17 ages 6–12, $5 age 5 and younger). Prepare to do a lot of quacking on the tour and to hear a lot of quackery regarding local history.

PARKS, PRESERVES, AND BEACHES

Greater Portland is blessed with green space, thanks largely to the efforts of 19th-century mayor James Phinney Baxter, who foresight-edly hired the famed Olmsted Brothers firm to develop an ambitious plan to ring the city with public parks and promenades. Not all the elements fell into place, but the result is what makes Portland such a livable city.

Portland Peninsula

Probably the most visible of the city's parks, 51-acre **Deering Oaks** (Park and Forest Aves. and Deering St.) may be best known for the quaint little duck condo in the middle of the pond. Other facilities and highlights here are tennis courts, playground, horseshoes, rental paddleboats, a snack bar, the award-winning Rose Circle, a Saturday farmers market (7 A.M.–noon), and, in winter, ice skating. After dark, steer clear of the park.

At one end of the Eastern Promenade, where it meets Fore Street, **Fort Allen Park** overlooks offshore Fort Gorges (coin-operated telescopes bring it closer). A central gazebo is flanked by an assortment of military souvenirs dating as far back as the War of 1812. All along the Eastern Prom are walking paths, benches, play areas, even an ill-maintained fitness trail—all with that terrific view. Down by the water is **East End Beach,** with parking, token sand, and the area's best launching ramp for sea kayaks or powerboats.

West of Downtown

Just beyond I-295, along Baxter Boulevard (Rte. 1) and tidal **Back Cove,** is a skinny green strip with a 3.5-mile trail for walking, jogging, or just watching the sailboards and the skyline. Along the way, you can cross Baxter Boulevard and spend time picnicking, playing tennis, or flying a kite in 48-acre **Payson Park.**

Talk about an urban oasis. The 85-acre **Fore River Sanctuary,** owned by Maine Audubon, has two miles of blue-blazed trails that wind through a salt marsh, link with the historic Cumberland and Oxford Canal towpath, and pass near **Jewell Falls,** Portland's only waterfall, protected by Portland Trails. From downtown Portland, take Congress Street West (Rte. 22), past I-295. From here there are two access routes: either turn right onto Stevens Avenue (Rte. 9), continue to Brighton Avenue (Rte. 25), turn left and go about 1.25 miles to Rowe Avenue, and then turn left and park at the end of the road; or continue past Stevens Avenue, about one-half mile to Frost Avenue, take a hard right, and then left into the Maine Orthopedic Center parking lot. Portland Trails raised the funds for the handsome, 90-foot pedestrian bridge at this entrance to the sanctuary. Open sunup to sundown daily. No pets, free admission.

Bird-watchers flock to 239-acre **Evergreen Cemetery** (Stevens Ave.) in May to see warblers, thrushes, and other migratory birds that gather in the ponds and meadows. During peak periods, it's possible to see as many as 20 warbler species in a morning, including the Cape May, bay breasted, mourning, and Tennessee. Naturalists from Maine Audubon often are on-site helping to identify birds. For more info, check the events calendar at www.Mainebirding.net.

Scarborough

Scarborough Beach Park (Black Point Rd., Rte. 207, 207/883-2416, www.scarborough-beachstatepark.com, $4 adult, $2 child), a long stretch of sand, is the best beach for big waves. Between the parking area and the lovely stretch of beach, you'll pass Massacre Pond, named for a 1703 skirmish between resident Indians and resident wannabes. (Score: Indians 19, wannabes 0.) The park is open all year for swimming, surfing, beachcombing, and ice skating, but on weekends in summer, the parking lot fills early.

At 3,100 acres, **Scarborough Marsh** (Pine Point Rd., Rte. 9, 207/883-5100, www.maine-audubon.org, 9:30 A.M.–5:30 P.M. June–Labor Day, and weekends in late May and Sept.), Maine's largest salt marsh, is prime territory for birding and canoeing. Rent a canoe ($15 an hour if you're not an Audubon member or $50 per half day) at the small nature center, operated by Maine Audubon, and explore on your own. Or join one of the daily 90-minute guided tours (call for the schedule, $11 adults, $9 children, subtract $1.50 pp if you have your own canoe). Guided full-moon tours ($12 per

adult, $10 per child) June–September are particularly exciting; dress warmly and bring a flashlight. Other special programs, some geared primarily for children, include wildflower walks, art classes, and dawn birding trips; all require reservations and very reasonable fees. Also here is a walking tour trail of less than one mile. Pick up a map at the center.

Overlooking the marsh is 52-acre **Scarborough River Wildlife Sanctuary** (Pine Point Rd./Rte. 9), with 1.5 miles of walking trails that loop to the Scarborough River and by two ponds.

Falmouth (North of Portland)

Nearly a dozen of Falmouth's parks, trails, and preserves, official and unofficial, are described and mapped in the *Falmouth Trail Guide,* a handy little booklet published by the Falmouth Conservation Commission. Copies are available at Gilsland Farm, Falmouth Town Hall,

© TOM NANGLE

When you need to stretch your legs, take a walk around Mackworth Island for a different view of the city skyline and Casco Bay.

and local bookstores. Two of the best options are described below.

A 65-acre wildlife sanctuary and environmental center on the banks of the Presumpscot River, **Gilsland Farm** (20 Gilsland Farm Rd., 207/781-2330, www.maineaudubon.org, dawn–dusk daily) is state headquarters for Maine Audubon. More than two miles of easy, well-marked trails wind through the grounds, taking in salt marshes, rolling meadows, woodlands, and views of the estuary. Observation blinds allow inconspicuous spying during bird-migration season. In the education center (9 A.M.–5 P.M. Mon.–Sat. and 1–4 P.M. Sun.) are hands-on exhibits, a nature store, and classrooms and offices. Fees are charged for special events, but otherwise it's all free. The visitors center is one-quarter mile off Route 1.

Once the summer compound of the prominent Baxter family, Falmouth's 100-acre **Mackworth Island,** reached via a causeway, is now the site of the Governor Baxter School for the Deaf. Limited parking is just beyond the security booth on the island. On the 1.5-mile, vehicle-free perimeter path (great Portland Harbor views), you'll meet bikers, hikers, and dog walkers. Just off the trail on the north side of the island is the late Governor Percival Baxter's stone-circled pet cemetery, maintained by the state at the behest of Baxter, who donated this island as well as Baxter State Park to the people of Maine. From downtown Portland, take Route 1 across the Presumpscot River to Falmouth Foreside. Andrews Avenue (third street on the right) leads to the island. Open sunup–sundown, all year.

RECREATION
Bicycling

The **Bicycle Coalition of Maine** (P.O. Box 5275, Augusta 04332, 207/623-4511, www.bikemaine.org) has an excellent website that lists nearly two dozen trails in Greater Portland. You'll also find info on events, organized rides, bike shops, and more. Another good resource is **Casco Bay Bicycle Club** (www.cascobaybicycleclub.org), a recreational cycling club with rides several times weekly. Check its website for details.

For rentals (hybrids are $25 a day) and repairs visit **Cycle Mania** (59 Federal St., 207/774-2933, www.cyclemania1.com).

The best locales for island bicycling—fun for families and beginners but not especially challenging for diehards—are Peaks and Great Chebeague Islands, but do remember to follow the rules of the road.

Golf

You'll have no problem finding a place to tee off in Greater Portland. Some of the best courses are private, so if you have an "in," so much the better, but there are still plenty of public and semiprivate courses for every skill level. Free advice on helping you choose a course is offered by Maine's Golf Concierge (info@golfme.com).

Let's just consider Greater Portland's 18-hole courses. For all, it's a smart move to reserve tee times. **Sable Oaks Golf Club** (505 Country Club Dr., South Portland, 207/775-6257, www.sableoaks.com) is considered one of the toughest and best of Maine's public courses. Since 1998, **Nonesuch River Golf Club** (304 Gorham Rd., Rte. 114, Scarborough, 207/883-0007 or 888/256-2717, www.nonesuchgolf.com) has been drawing raves for the challenges of its par-70 championship course and praise from environmentalists for preserving wildlife habitat; full-size practice range and green, too. The City of Portland's **Riverside Municipal Golf Course** (1158 Riverside St., Portland, 207/797-3524) has an 18-hole par-72 course (Riverside North) and a nine-hole par-35 course (Riverside South). Opt for the 18-hole course.

Sea Kayaking

With all the islands scattered through Casco Bay, Greater Portland has become a hotbed of sea-kayaking activity. The best place to start is out on Peaks Island, 15 minutes offshore via Casco Bay Lines ferry. **Maine Island Kayak Company (MIKCO)** (70 Luther St., Peaks Island, 207/766-2373 or 800/796-2373, www.maineislandkayak.com) is a successful tour operation that organizes half-day, all-day,

Maine Island Kayak Company operates from a beachfront location on Peaks Island, making it easy to tour the waters of Casco Bay.

and multiday local kayaking trips as well as national and international adventures. An introductory half-day tour in Casco Bay is $65 pp; a full day is $110, including lunch. Reservations are essential. MIKCO also does private lessons and group courses and clinics (some require previous experience). MIKCO's owner, Tom Bergh, has a flawless reputation for safety and skill. Send for the extensive trip schedule. In early October (usually Columbus Day weekend), there's a daylong sale of used boats and gear—lots of real bargains.

For a quickie intro, **L. L. Bean** (180 Commercial St., 207/400-4814) offers 90-minute Portland Harbor kayak tours three times daily late June–August, and then weekends into October. Cost is $29 adults, $19 ages 10–15.

ⓒ Lobstering Cruise

Learn all kinds of lobster lore and maybe even catch your own dinner with **Lucky Catch Lobster Tours** (170 Commercial St., 207/233-2026 or 888/624-6321, www.lucky-catch.com, $22 adult, $20 seniors or juniors ages 13–18, $14 ages 12 and younger). Captain

Tom Martin offers five different, 80–90-minute cruises on his 37-foot lobster boat. On each (except late Saturdays and all-day Sundays, when state law prohibits it), usually 10 traps are hauled and the process and gear explained. You can even help, if you're willing. Any lobsters caught are available for purchase after the cruise for wholesale boat price (and you can have them cooked nearby for a reasonable rate). Now wouldn't that make a nice story to tell the folks back home?

Sailboat and Powerboat Excursions

Down on the Old Port wharves are several excursion-boat businesses. Each has carved out a niche, so choose according to your interest and your schedule. Dress warmly and wear rubber-soled shoes. Remember that all cruises are weather-dependent.

Bay View Cruises operates the 66-foot *Bay View Lady* (184 Commercial St., Fisherman's Wharf, Old Port, 207/761-0496, www.bayviewcruises-me.com, daily June–Sept., weekends May and June) and has five different cruises ranging from 40 minutes to two hours. On longer cruises, you can add a complete lobster bake, with notice. The main deck is enclosed and heated; the upper deck has the best views.

Cruise up to 20 miles offshore seeking whales with **Odyssey Whale Watch** (Long Wharf, 170 Commercial St., 207/775-0727, www.odysseywhalewatch.com, $40 adult, $35 ages 60-plus and 13–17, and $30 under 12). Five-hour whale watches aboard the *Odyssey* depart daily at 10 A.M. late June–early September, plus spring and fall weekends. (Don't overload on breakfast that day, and take preventive measures if you're motion-sensitive.)

Eagle Island Tours (Long Wharf, Old Port, 207/774-6498, www.eagleisland-tours.com, no credit cards) offers several excursion options, but the best is the four-hour cruise, departing at 10 A.M., to 17-acre **Eagle Island** (Tues. and Thurs.–Sun. late June–early Sept., and some weekends June and September, $26 adults, $24 seniors, $14 ages 3–12) where Arctic explorer Admiral Robert Peary built his summer home. The cruise allows time on the island to visit the house and wander the grounds. Pack a picnic, or order a box lunch 24 hours in advance.

Sail quietly across the waters of Casco Bay aboard a windjammer with **Portland Schooner Company** (Maine State Pier, 40 Commercial St., 207/766-2500, www.portlandschooner.com, late May–mid-Oct., $30 adult, $15 ages 2–12). Three or four two-hour sails are offered daily on two schooners, the 72-foot *Bagheera* and the 88-foot *Wendameen,* both historical vessels designed by John G. Alden and built in East Boothbay. Overnight windjammer trips also are available for $240 pp, including dinner and breakfast.

Spectator Sports

A pseudofierce mascot named Slugger stirs up the crowds at baseball games played by the **Portland Sea Dogs** (Hadlock Field, 271 Park Ave., 207/879-9500 or 800/936-3647, www.portlandseadogs.com), a AA Boston Red Sox farm team. Ever since the team arrived, in 1994, loyal local fans have made tickets

scarce, so it's wise to reserve well ahead (you'll pay a minimal reservation surcharge) with a major credit card. The season schedule (early Apr.–Aug.) is available after January 1. General-admission tickets are $6 adults, $3 seniors (62 and over) and kids 16 and under. Reserved seats are $7 adults, $6 all others.

For ice hockey action, the **Portland Pirates** (207/775-3458, www.portlandpirates.com, $8–21), a farm team for the American Hockey League Anaheim Ducks, plays winter and spring home games at the 8,700-seat Cumberland County Civic Center.

The civic center is also the locale for year-round special sporting events and exhibition games, and ice shows, concerts, and college hockey games. Check the *Portland Press Herald* for schedules or call the center.

ENTERTAINMENT AND NIGHTLIFE

The best places to find out what's playing at area theaters, cinemas, concert halls, and nightclubs are the *The Portland Phoenix* and the *Go* supplement in the Thursday edition of the *Portland Press Herald.* Both are available at bookstores and supermarkets; the *Phoenix* is free.

Merrill Auditorium

The magnificently restored Merrill Auditorium (20 Myrtle St., box office 207/874-8200) is a 1,900-seat theater inside Portland City Hall (on Congress Street) with two balconies and one of the country's only municipally owned pipe organs, the **Kotzschmar Organ.** A summer organ classical concert series with guest artists is held at 7:30 P.M. most Tuesdays mid-June–August, $10 donation. Call for more information on the Pops series (207/883-9525).

Special events and concerts are common at Merrill, and the auditorium is also the home to a number of the city's arts organizations. The **Portland Symphony Orchestra** (207/842-0800, www.portlandsymphony.org) and **PCA Great Performances** (207/773-3150, www.pcagreatperformances.org) have extensive, well-patronized fall and winter schedules; the PSO presents three summer

Independence Pops concerts as well. The **Portland Opera Repertory Theatre** (437 Congress St., 207/879-7678, www.portopera.org) performs a major opera each summer, usually in late July. In addition, there are films, lectures, and other related events throughout July. Tickets for the PSO, PCA, and PORT are available through PortTix (207/942-0800, www.porttix.com).

St. Lawrence Arts and Community Center

Proof of what enthusiastic, determined activists can accomplish is the new St. Lawrence Arts and Community Center (76 Congress St., 207/775-5568, www.stlawrencearts.org), formerly St. Lawrence Congregational Church. Built in 1897 in Queen Anne style, the church is a distinctive landmark with more than 90 stained-glass windows. On the same street as the Portland Observatory on Munjoy Hill, the center is a vibrant venue for professional and semiprofessional theater and concerts.

1 Longfellow Square

The former Center for Cultural Exchange has been reborn as 1 Longfellow Square (207/761-1257, www.onelongfellowsquare.com), a venue for performances and lectures at the corner of Congress and State Streets.

Drama

Innovative staging and controversial contemporary dramas are typical of the **Portland Stage Company** (Portland Performing Arts Center, 25A Forest Ave., 207/774-0465, www.portlandstage.com), established in 1974 and going strong ever since. Equity pros present a half dozen plays each winter season in a 290-seat performance space.

Live Music

The Portland Conservatory of Music presents the free, weekly **Noonday Concerts** at First Parish Church (425 Congress St., 207/773-5747) at 12:15 P.M. Thursdays October–early April (excluding late November). The music varies widely, from saxophone to Scottish fiddle and dance, a string quartet to Irish baroque.

Portland Parks and Recreation sponsors **Summer in the Parks** (207/756-8275, www.ci.portland.me.us/summer.htm, July and Aug., free), a number of evening concert series, a noontime kids' series, and even movies, in downtown parks.

In summer, take the ferry to Peaks Island for sunset cocktails and often live entertainment on the deck at **Jones Landing** (at the ferry landing, Peaks Island, 207/766-4400).

Brewpubs and Bars

Not only is **Gritty McDuff's** (396 Fore St., Old Port, 207/772-2739, 11:30 A.M.–1 A.M. daily) one of Maine's most popular breweries, its brewpub was the state's first—opened in 1988. The menu includes pub classics such as fish-and-chips and shepherd's pie, as well as burgers, salads, and sandwiches. Among the Gritty's beers and ales on tap are Sebago Light and Black Fly Stout. Gritty's also books live entertainment fairly regularly. Tours by appointment. Gritty's also has a branch in Freeport.

Sebago Brewing Company (164 Middle St., Old Port, 207/775-2337, 11:30 A.M.–1 A.M. daily) is newer on the scene, but prolific, with brewpubs also in Gorham and at the Maine Mall. The Portland location has seating indoors and out and a menu that varies from munchies to steak and lobster. Tours on request.

A longtime favorite pub, **$3 Dewey's** (241 Commercial St., Old Port, 207/772-3310) is so authentic that visiting Brits, Kiwis, and Aussies often head here to assuage their homesickness. Inexpensive fare, 36 brews on tap, free popcorn, and live music on Sunday, Tuesday, Wednesday, and Thursday make it a very popular spot.

Especially popular in the late afternoon and early evening is **J's Oyster** (5 Portland Pier, 207/772-4828, 11:30 A.M.–1 A.M.), a longtime fixture on the waterfront known for its raw bar and for pouring a good drink.

Of all Portland's neighborhood hangouts, **Ruski's** (212 Danforth St., 207/774-7604,

7 A.M.–12:45 A.M. Mon.–Sat., 9 A.M.–12:45 A.M. Sun.) is the most authentic—a small, usually crowded onetime speakeasy that rates just as high for breakfast as for nighttime schmoozing. Expect basic, homemade fare for well under $10, darts and big-screen TV, too. Dress down or you'll feel out of place. No credit cards.

That said, it's **Rosie's** (330 Fore St., 207/772-5656) that *Esquire* named as one of America's best bars. **Blackstones** (6 Pine St., 207/775-2885, www.blackstones.com) claims to be Portland's oldest neighborhood gay bar.

West of I-295, **The Great Lost Bear** (540 Forest Ave., 207/772-0300, www.greatlostbear.com, 11:30 A.M.–11:30 P.M. Mon.–Sat., noon–11 P.M. Sun.) has Portland's hugest inventory of designer beers, with 54 brews on tap, representing 15 Maine microbreweries and others from New England. The bear motif and the punny menus are a bit much, but the 15 or so varieties of burgers are not bad. It's a kid pleaser.

For more upscale tippling, head for **Top of the East** (157 High St., near Congress Sq., 207/775-5411), the lounge at the top of the Eastland Park Hotel, where all of Portland's at your feet. Happy hour is 4–6 P.M. weekdays; the lounge is open until 1 A.M. Thursday–Saturday, midnight other nights. Live jazz begins at 9:30 P.M. Friday and Saturday. **Una** (505 Fore St., 207/828-0300) is a hip cocktail and wine bar serving a tapas-style menu. Another longtime favorite is **The Wine Bar** (38 Wharf St., 207/773-6667).

Bars with Entertainment

So many possibilities are in this category, but not a lot of veterans. The Portland club scene is a volatile one, tough on investors and reporters. The best advice is to scope out the scene when you arrive; the *Portland Phoenix* has the best listings. Most clubs have cover charges. A sampling of some Portland options follows. **Asylum** (121 Center St., 207/772-8274, www.portlandasylum.com) caters to a young crowd with dance jams, CD release parties, DJ nights, and live bands. **Geno's** (13 Brown St., 207/772-7891) has been at it for

years—an old reliable for rock, with an emphasis on punk rock. **Brian Boru** (57 Center St., Old Port, 207/780-1506, www.bboru.com) is an Irish pub with live Irish music and $2 pints of Guinness on Sundays. Another venue for live music is **The Big Easy** (55 Market St., 207/871-8817, www.bigeasyportland.com). **Blue** (650A Congress St., 207/774-4111, www.portcityblue.com) presents local artists and musicians in a small space and serves beer, wine, tea, and light fare; traditional Irish music is always featured on Wednesday evenings, jazz on Saturdays. Another *Esquire* recommendation is **The White Heart** (551 Congress St., 207/828-1900), a hip cocktail lounge with live music on weekends and often a DJ midweek.

Comedy

Portland's forum for stand-up comedy is the **Comedy Connection** (6 Custom House Wharf, 207/774-5554, www.mainecomedy.com, open Thurs.–Sun. evenings), a crowded space that draws nationally known pros. Avoid the front tables unless you're inclined to be the fall guy/guinea pig, and don't bring anyone squeamish about the F-word. Bring your sense of humor, enjoy the show, and patronize the waitstaff; they have a tough job. Reservations advised on weekends.

EVENTS

Pick up a free copy of the *Portland Area Arts and Events Calendar* at Portland shops and cafés, the Visitor Information Center, or City Hall (389 Congress St.).

June brings a host of events. The **Old Port Festival** (one of Portland's largest festivals), usually the first weekend, has entertainment, food and craft booths, and impromptu fun in Portland's Old Port. The **Greek Heritage Festival,** usually the last weekend, features Greek food, dancing, and crafts at Holy Trinity Church (133 Pleasant St., Portland).

Some of the world's top runners join upward of 500 racers in the **Beach to Beacon Race,** held in late July/early August. The 10K course goes from Crescent Beach State Park to Portland Head Light in Cape Elizabeth.

In mid-August, the **Italian Street Festival** showcases music, Italian food, and games at St. Peter's Catholic Church (72 Federal St.).

Artists from all over the country set up in 350 booths along Congress Street for the annual **Sidewalk Arts Festival,** in late August.

The **Maine Brewers' Festival,** the first weekend in November at the Portland Exposition Building, is a big event that expands every year, thanks to the explosion of Maine microbreweries. Samples galore. And from Thanksgiving weekend to Christmas Eve, **Victorian Holiday,** in downtown Portland, harks back with caroling, special sales, concerts, tree lighting, horse-drawn wagons, and Victoria Mansion tours and festivities.

SHOPPING

The Portland peninsula—primarily Congress Street and the Old Port waterfront district—is thick with non-cookie-cutter shops and galleries. This is just a taste to spur your explorations.

Bookstores

Carlson-Turner Books (241 Congress St., 207/773-4200 or 800/540-7323), based on Munjoy Hill, seems to have Portland's largest used-book inventory. Look for unusual titles and travel narratives. For good reads, contemporary fiction, and a big selection of cookbooks, visit **Cunningham Books** (199 State St., Longfellow Sq., 207/775-2246). Antique maps and atlases are the specialty at the Old Port's **Emerson Booksellers** (18 Exchange St., 207/874-2665), but it also has an excellent used-book selection.

Cookbook mavens will drool over the collection at **Rabelais Books** (86 Market St., 207/774-1044, www.rabelaisbooks.com), ideally situated in Portland's foodie neighborhood. Don and Samantha Hoyt Lindgren specialize in food and wine, carrying a delicious blend of thousands of current, rare, and out-of-print books covering culinary history, food lit, cookbooks, wine, and related topics.

For current works, **Books Etc.** (38 Exchange St., 207/774-0626) is a independent shop with a wide-ranging inventory.

Art Galleries

Intown Portland's galleries host a **First Friday Artwalk** on the first Friday evening of each month, with exhibition openings, open houses, meet-the-artist gatherings, and other such artsy activities.

A handful of galleries specializing in contemporary art are clustered in the Arts District. These include **Aucocisco** (613 Congress St., 207/553-2222, www.aucocisco.com), **June Fitzpatrick Gallery** (112 High St., 207/879-5742, www.junefitzpatrickgallery.com), and **Institute for Contemporary Art** (Maine College of Art, 522 Congress St., 207/879-5742), with walk-in tours at 12:15 P.M. every Wednesday. In the Old Port, find **Greenhut Galleries** (146 Middle St., 207/772-2693, www.greenhutgalleries.com), another well-respected gallery showing contemporary Maine art and sculpture.

Crafts

More than 15 Maine potters—with a wide variety of styles and items—market their wares at the **Maine Potters Market** (376 Fore St., 207/774-1633), an attractive shop in the heart of the Old Port. Established in 1980, the cooperative remains a consistently reliable outlet for some of Maine's best ceramic artisans.

Just around the corner is **Abacus** (44 Exchange St., 207/772-4880), where craft rises to a high art. Whimsy is the byword here; if you don't arrive smiling, you'll leave that way. Open all year. Abacus has branches in Kennebunkport and Freeport, and a seasonal shop in Boothbay Harbor.

Offbeat Shopping

Trustmi, you have to see **Suitsmi** (35 Pleasant St., 207/772-8285, www.suitsmi.com), which carries wearables (including jewelry) perfect for rock concerts, funky cafés, and, if you're dying to make a statement, your class reunion. Top it all off with a hat from **Queen of Hats** (560

Congress St., 207/772-2379, www.queenofhats.com). **Shipwreck and Cargo** (207 Commercial St., Old Port, 207/775-3057, www.shipwreckandcargo.com) stocks a wide assortment of marine-related items—boat models, barometers, navy surplus stuff, and more. Even more fun and offbeat is **China Sea Marine Trading Co.** (Wharf St., 207/773-0081, www.chinaseatrading.com), where Steve Bunker and his macaw Singapore sell his wild and eclectic finds.

Woof. The company outlet **Planet Dog** (211 Marginal Way, Portland, 207/347-8606, www.planetdog.com) is a barking good time for dogs and their owners. You'll find all sorts of wonderful products, and Planet Dog, committed to "think globally and act doggedly," has established a foundation to promote and serve causes such as therapy, service, search and rescue, bomb sniffing, and police dogs.

ACCOMMODATIONS
Downtown Portland

Portland's peninsula doesn't have an overwhelming amount of sleeping space, but it does have good variety in all price ranges. Rates reflect peak season.

Inns/Bed-and-Breakfasts: Railroad tycoon John Deering built **The Inn at St. John** (939 Congress St., 207/773-6481 or 800/636-9127, www.innatstjohn.com, $85–180) in 1897. The clean, comfortable, moderately priced 37-room hostelry has the feel of a European-style hotel. It welcomes children and pets and even has bicycle storage. Cable TV, air-conditioning, free local calls, free parking, free airport pickup, and continental breakfast are provided. Most rooms have private baths (some are detached); some have fridge and microwave. The only downsides are the lack of an elevator and the lackluster neighborhood—in the evening you'll want drive or take a taxi when going out. It's about a half-hour walk to the Old Port or an $8 taxi fare.

Staying at ◖ **The Pomegranate Inn** (49 Neal St. at Carroll St., 207/772-1006 or 800/356-0408, www.pomegranateinn.com, $175–285) is an adventure in itself, with faux painting, classical statuary, art, antiques, and whimsical touches everywhere—you'll either love it or find it a bit much. The elegant 1884 Italianate mansion has seven guest rooms and a suite, all with private baths, air-conditioning, TV, and phones, some with fireplaces. Afternoon refreshments are served.

Take an 1830s townhouse, add contemporary amenities and a service-oriented innkeeper, and the result is the **Morrill Mansion Bed and Breakfast** (249 Vaughan St., 207/774-6900 or 888/566-7745, www.morrillmansion.com, $189–219), on the West End. Six rooms and one suite are spread out on the second and third floors (no elevator) in a carefully renovated town house. No frilly Victorian accents here—rather, the decor is understated, yet tasteful, taking advantage of hardwood floors and high ceilings. You'll find free Wi-Fi and local calls and TV/DVD in each room. A continental breakfast is included; off-street parking is free. It's near the hospital, so you might hear a siren or two. The only real negative is the lack of a comfortable living room–type area.

Former travel writer Dale Northrup put his experience to work in opening the **Percy Inn** (15 Pine St., 207/871-7638 or 888/417-3729, www.percyinn.com, $119–199), just off Longfellow Square. You can easily hole up in the guest rooms, which are furnished with phones, fax machines, CD players, TVs with VCRs, wet bars, and stocked refrigerators, and they have air-condtioning. It's best suited for independent-minded travelers who don't desire much contact with the host or other guests, as public rooms are few and the innkeeper is rarely onsite. Breakfast is a continental buffet.

Built in 1835, **The Inn at Park Spring** (135 Spring St., 207/774-1059 or 800/427-8511, www.innatparkspring.com, $149–175) is one of Portland's longest-running B&Bs. Current innkeepers Nancy and John Gonsalves are adding their own touches to make guests feel right at home. The location is just steps from most Arts District attractions. Six guest rooms are spread out on three floors (no elevator, steep stairs). All have air-conditioning and phones, some have Internet access; one has a private patio and entrance. There's a guest fridge on each floor. Rates include a full breakfast.

Built in 1877, the handsome Georgian-style **The West End Inn** (146 Pine St. at Neal St., 207/772-1377 or 800/338-1377, www.westendbb.com, $159–209) has six nicely decorated second- and third-floor guest rooms with TV, and a first-floor room with private porch. A full breakfast is served. Pack light if you're on the third floor.

Full-Service Hotels: You might have trouble finding the **The Portland Regency** (20 Milk St., 207/774-4200 or 800/727-3436, www.theregency.com, $199–249). That's because this lovely hotel is secreted in a renovated armory in the heart of the Old Port. Local calls are free, Wi-Fi and laptop rentals are available, and free shuttles are provided to all major Portland transportation facilities. Room configurations vary widely—some provide little natural window light or are strangely shaped. All have 27-inch TVs, minibars, and air-conditioning. A restaurant, spa, and fitness center are on-site.

Newest and most luxurious is the **⟨ Portland Harbor Hotel** (468 Fore St., 207/775-9090 or 888/798-9090, www.portlandharborhotel.com, $249–379), an upscale, boutique hotel in the Old Port built around a garden courtyard. Rooms are plush, with chic linens, duvets, down pillows on the beds, Wi-Fi and digital cable TV, and bathrooms with separate soaking tubs and showers. Bike rentals are available for $15 per day, and the hotel offers a free local car service. The restaurant is excellent. The downside is that the neighborhood can be noisy at night, so request a room facing the interior courtyard, preferably on the upper floors.

Yes, it's a chain, and yes, it's downright ugly, but the **Holiday Inn by the Bay** (88 Spring St., 207/775-2311 or 800/345-5050, www.innbythebay.com, $176–188) provides a lot of bang for the buck. It's conveniently situated between the waterfront and the Arts District; rooms on upper floors have views either over Back Cove or Portland Harbor; Wi-Fi and parking are free as is a shuttle service. It also has an in-door pool, sauna, and fitness room and on-site laundry facilities, in addition to a restaurant and lounge.

Beyond Downtown

South of Portland are a number of inns and resorts, some right on the ocean, others within walking distance.

Just down the street from neighborhoody Higgins Beach is the informal **Higgins Beach Inn** (34 Ocean Ave., Scarborough, 207/883-6684 or 800/836-2322, www.higginsbeachinn.com, mid-May–mid-Oct., $125–165), what your mind's eye might conjure as a traditional, turn-of-the-20th-century summer hotel. It has 24 no-frills rooms, some with shared bath, a few with ocean views. The inn's **Garofalo's Restaurant** has a creative Italian slant, emphasizing seafood (entrées $18–26). In summer, the restaurant is open to the public for breakfast 7:30–10:30 A.M. and dinner 5–9 P.M.; reservations are advisable for dinner, especially on weekends.

In 2007, the **Black Point Inn Resort** (510 Black Point Rd., Prouts Neck, Scarborough, 207/883-2500 or 800/258-0003, www.blackpointinn.com, $190–289 pp, including breakfast, afternoon tea, and dinner) reopened after being dramatically downsized and upscaled. The historical shingle-style hotel sits at the tip of Prouts Neck, with views to Casco Bay from one side and down to Old Orchard from the other, and beaches out the front and back doors. Now owned by a local partnership, the inn has returned to its roots, catering to wealthy rusticators. The Point dining room is open to the public by reservation (6–9 P.M. daily, $19–38), but first, have cocktails on the porch at sunset. Staying here is splurge worthy. Guests have access to a private 18-hole golf course and tennis courts.

Seven miles south of downtown Portland, **Inn by the Sea** (40 Bowery Beach Rd., Rte. 77, Cape Elizabeth, 207/799-3134 or 800/888-4287, www.innbythesea.com, $399–789 d) is a well-managed modern complex with the stylishly casual feel of an upscale summerhouse. It underwent a major renovation and expansion

GREATER PORTLAND

(reopening June 2008) that added a full-service spa and cardio room. Guests stay in hotel rooms, spa suites, or two-bedroom garden cottages, all with spectacular water views. A boardwalk winds down through the salt marsh to the southern end of Crescent Beach State Park. Facilities include an outdoor pool and croquet lawn. By reservation, pets are honored guests here (they even have their own room-service menu). Make reservations early; the inn is incredibly popular. Priceless Audubon prints cover the walls in the appropriately named **Audubon Room** (207/767-0888), where moderate-to-expensive breakfasts, lunches, and dinners are served daily to guests—and to the public by reservation.

The **Peter A. McKernan Hospitality Center** (Southern Maine Technical College, Fort Rd., South Portland, front desk 207/741-5672, reservations 207/741-5662, www.hospitality.smccme.edu, $175) provides a different twist on the inn experience. In fact, it's the proving ground for students in the Lodging and Restaurant Management Program at Southern Maine Community College. The center, a 1902 brick building that once served as officers' quarters, has spectacular views of Casco Bay and the offshore islands. Students staff the inn, and they all aim to please. Shorefront walking/biking trails are nearby. The center keeps a low profile, yet rooms are booked far ahead. Rates include continental breakfast.

Island Lodging

The **Inn on Peaks Island** (33 Island Ave., www.theinnonpeaksisland.com, $250–300) overlooks the ferry dock and has jaw-dropping sunset views over the Portland skyline. No island roughing it here. The spacious cottage-style guest rooms have fireplaces, sitting areas, whirlpool baths, TV and VCR, refrigerators, and rates include a continental breakfast. Lunch and dinner are also served in the inn's Shipyard Brewhaus restaurant ($10–22). Access is via Casco Bay Lines or a water taxi.

On the other end of the Peaks Island luxury scale is the extremely informal and communal **Eighth Maine Living Museum and Lodge** (13 Eighth Maine Ave., 207/766-5086 mid-May–mid-Sept., 914/237-3165 off-season, $80–100), a shorefront, rustic, living history lodge overlooking White Head Passage. Shared baths and a huge shared kitchen (in which every room is allocated a two-burner gas stove, cabinet space, dining table, and access to full kitchen facilities) allow you to rusticate in much the same manner as did the Civil War vets who built this place, in 1891, with a gift from a veteran who had won the Louisiana Lottery. It has no housekeeping—you're responsible for stripping the linens and cleaning the room and your kitchen space before departing.

The **Chebeague Orchard Inn** (453 North Rd., Chebeague Island, 207/846-9488, $125–165) doubles as longtime residents Vickie and Neil Taliento's comfortable, antiques-filled home. Five rooms have handmade quilts (three have private baths and two share a bath); some have water views. The congenial Talientos are big supporters of the Maine Island Trail Association, so you'll get a discount if you arrive by kayak (the trail begins near Chebeague). Coffee's ready at 7 A.M.; breakfast is continental midweek, full on the weekends and served overlooking the backyard's bird feeders and apple orchard. There are bikes for guests, a fireplace in the common room, and tons of helpful advice about the island. For dinner, many guests pick up takeout and bring it back to the inn.

Another possibility might be the **Chebeague Island Inn,** a lovely and historical inn with a dining room that was expected to reopen once it's sold.

FOOD

Downtown Portland alone has more than 100 restaurants, so it's impossible to list even all the great ones—and there are many. The city's proximity to fresh foods, from both farms and the sea, makes it popular with chefs, and its Italian roots and growing immigrant population mean a good choice of ethnic dining, too. Below is a choice selection, by neighborhood, with open days and hours provided for peak season. Call in advance September–

June. You'll note that some restaurants don't list a closing time; that's because they shut the doors when the crowd thins, so call ahead if you're heading out much after 8 P.M., just to be safe. Do make reservations, whenever possible, and as far in advance as you can, especially in July and August. If you're especially into the food scene, check www.portlandfoodmap.com for a breakdown by cuisine of Portland restaurants with links to recent reviews.

If you'll be in Maine for more than a few days, check out the **Portland Dine Around Club** (P.O. Box 15338, Portland 04112, 207/775-4711 or 877/732-2582, www.dineportland.com, $29.95). This discount card gets you two-for-the-price-of-one meals (usually dinner entrées) at more than 150 restaurants with a wide variety of menus, decor, and price ranges as well as discounts at numerous attractions, museums, performing arts venues, and even lodging, statewide. Check the website to see if the discounts are valid where and when you want them.

In addition to the many restaurant options listed here, check the *Community News* listings in each Wednesday's *Portland Press Herald*. Under "Potluck," you'll find listings of **public meals,** usually benefiting nonprofit organizations. Prices are always quite low (under $10 for adults, $2–4 for children), mealtimes quite early (5 or 6 P.M.), and the flavor quite local.

When you need a java fix, **Coffee by Design** (620 Congress St., 67 India St., and 43 Washington Ave.) is the local choice, not only for its fine brews but also for its support of local artists and community causes.

The Portland Farmers Market sets up on Wednesdays on Monument Square and on Saturdays in Deering Oaks Park.

The Old Port and the Waterfront

All of these are east of the Franklin Street Arterial, between Congress and Commercial Streets.

Best known for the earliest and most filling breakfast, **Becky's Diner** (Hobson's Wharf, 390 Commercial St., Old Port, 207/773-7070, 4 A.M.–9 P.M. daily) has more than a dozen om-

elette choices, just for a start. It also serves lunch and dinner, all at downright cheap prices.

The color's a lot more local just down the street at **The Porthole** (20 Custom House Wharf, Commercial St., Old Port, 207/774-6652, 7 A.M.–2 A.M. Mon.–Sat.), a onetime dive that's been gussied up a bit. The all-you-can-eat Friday fish fry pulls in *real* fishermen, in-the-know locals, and fearless tourists. Eat inside or on the wharf. I like it for breakfast or the Friday $5.95 all-you-can-eat fish fry.

Pizza with a view is on tap at **Flatbread Company** (72 Commercial St., 207/772-8777, www.flatbreadcompany.com, 11:30 A.M.–10 P.M. daily), part of a small, New England chain. The all-natural pizza is baked in a primitive, wood-fired clay oven and served in a dining room with a wall of windows overlooking the ferry terminal and Portland Harbor. Half- and whole-size pizzas include choices such as nitrate-free pepperoni, vegan (dairy-free) flatbread, cheese and herb, and you-choose combos.

Healthful fast food? Stonyfield Farm CEO Gary Hirshberg proved it wasn't an oxymoron with **O'Natural's** (88 Exchange St., 207/321-2050, www.onaturals.com, 7:30 A.M.–8 P.M., to 8:30 P.M. Fri. and Sat., 10 A.M.–3 P.M. Sun.). The emphasis is on fresh, local, and organic, with choices including flatbread sandwiches, tossed salads, Asian noodles, soups, and even a kids' menu. Wheat-free, dairy-free, and veggie choices are available. It's all served in a historical bank building, where the huge safe is now a safe play area for kids.

For "gourmet goodies" don't miss **Browne Trading Market** (Merrill's Wharf, 262 Commercial St., 207/775-7560). Owner Rod Mitchell became the Caviar King of Portland by wholesaling Caspian caviar, and he's now letting the rest of us in on it. Ultimately fresh fish and shellfish fill the cases next to the caviar and cheeses. The mezzanine is wall-to-wall (literally) wine, specializing in French.

Sweet Treats: When you're craving carbs, want pastries for breakfast, or need to boost your energy with a sweet, follow your nose to **Standard Baking Company** (75 Commercial

St., 207/773-2112), deservedly famous for its handcrafted breads and pastries. Chocoholics take note: When a craving strikes for scrumptious homemade chocolates or ice cream, head to **Fuller's** (Wharf St., 207/253-8010).

Fish and Seafood: Ask around, and everyone will tell you the best seafood in town is at **Street and Company** (33 Wharf St., Old Port, 207/775-0887, 5–9:30 P.M., to 10 P.M. Fri. and Sat.). Fresh, beautifully prepared fish (entrées begin about $18) is what you get, often with a Mediterranean flair. Tables are tight, and it's often noisy in the informal, brick-walled rooms.

If that's a little too limited, consider **Old Port Sea Grille and Raw Bar** (www.theoldportseagrill.com, opens 11:30 A.M. daily), a sleek, modern spot near the waterfront, with a fabulous raw bar and 500-gallon aquarium inside. Entrées run $20–33, and no surprise, seafood is the specialty.

For lobster in the rough, head to **Portland Lobster Company** (180 Commercial St., 207/775-2112, 11 A.M.–9 P.M. daily). There's a small inside seating area, but it's much more pleasant to sit out on the wharf and watch the excursion boats come and go. Expect to pay in the low $20 range for a one-pound lobster with fries and slaw. Other choices ($8–23) and a kids' menu are available.

Ethnic Fare: Be forewarned: Your first foray into (**Bresca** (111 Middle St., 207/772-1004, opens 5:30 P.M. Tues.–Sat.) won't be your last. Chef Krista Kerns delivers big flavor in this small, Italian-flavored space next to Portland's police station. She shops each morning, buying just enough for that night's meal (yes, items do sell out). You'll need a reservation to land one of the 20 seats. Service is personal, the meal is leisurely, the food divine. Do save room for dessert: Krista initially made her name as a pastry chef.

Top-notch for northern Italian is **Cinque Terre Ristorante** (36 Wharf St., 207/347-6154, www.cinqueterremaine.com, 5–9 P.M. Sun.–Thurs., to 10 P.M. Fri. and Sat.). Chef Lee Skawinski is committed to sustainable farming, and much of the seasonal and organic

produce used comes from the restaurant owners' Laughing Stock Farm and other Maine farms. The restaurant is housed in a former ship's chandlery that's been transformed into a comfortable, Tuscan-accented dining area, with an open kitchen and seating either on the main floor or a second-floor balcony that rims the open space. Choose from half- or full-size portions ranging $12–28. Do begin with the antipasto plate, and don't miss the handmade pastas or the lobster risotto. More than 100 Italian wines are on the award-winning list. Service can be iffy.

Cinque Terre's sister restaurant, **Vignola** (10 Dana St., 207/772-1330, www.vignolamaine .com, 11 A.M.–2:30 P.M. and 5 P.M.–midnight daily, opens 10 A.M. Sun. for brunch), is more casual and less pricey ($10–18) and wins points for late-night dining.

Ask locally about **Village Café,** an ever-popular family favorite for its respectable Italian food (entrées $10–23), healthful specials, and fried clams. In biz since 1936, it expected to reopen in a new Portland location in 2008.

Irish fare with a Maine accent fills the menu at **Ri-Ra** (72 Commercial St., Old Port, 207/761-4446, www.rira.com, 11:30 A.M.–10 P.M. daily). How about beef stew made with Guinness? Or grilled salmon with leeks? Entrées in the glass-walled second-floor dining room (overlooking the Casco Bay Lines ferry terminal) are $11–29. Appetizers and desserts are superb, too. The ground-floor pub, elegantly woody, with an enormous bar, is inevitably stuffed to the gills on weekends—a great spot for such traditional fare as corned beef and cabbage (pub entrées $8–16) as long as you can stand the din. No reservations, so be prepared to wait, especially on weekends.

Eclectic Dining: The people-watching can't be beat from the patio or deck of **Mims Brasserie** (205 Commercial St., Old Port, 207/345-7478, www.mimsportland.com, 8 A.M.–9:30 P.M. Mon.–Fri., 9 A.M.–10 P.M. Sat.–Sun.). The à la carte French-inspired menu features naturally raised meats. Dinner entrées are $12–25; side dishes are extra and designed to be mixed, matched, and shared. Create your own omelette at breakfast; Benedicts are the specialties during weekend brunch.

One of Portland's old reliables, **Walter's** (15 Exchange St., 207/871-9258, www.walterscafe.com, 11 A.M.–2:30 P.M. and 5–9 P.M., no lunch Sun.) has been serving creative fusion fare since 1990s, and despite the longevity, it's never tiresome. The two-level dining room can be noisy. Entrées run around $16–26.

Okay, it's not exactly on the city's waterfront, but you take a Casco Bay Lines ferry from there to get to **Diamond's Edge Restaurant** (Great Diamond Island, 207/766-5850, www.diamondsedge.com, 11:30 A.M.–2:30 P.M. and 5–9 P.M. daily late May–late Sept.). You'll need to coordinate your dining with the ferry schedule, but it's worth it for the views along the way. Best bet: Go for lunch. The restaurant, in a renovated Fort McKinley Quartermaster Corps building, is elegant without being at all stuffy. In fine weather, you can dine outside.

Destination Dining: Plan well in advance to get a reservation at **€ Fore Street** (288 Fore St., Old Port, 207/775-2717, www.forestreet.biz, 5:30–10 P.M. Sun.–Thurs., to 10:30 P.M. Fri. and Sat.). Chef Sam Hayward, a fixture on the Maine food scene who is well known for his creative use of Maine-sourced ingredients, won the James Beard Award for Best Chef in the Northeast in 2004 and has been featured in most of the foodie publications. Even though the copper-topped tables, open kitchen, and the industrial decor create a din in this ex-warehouse, no one seems to mind much. Game is roasted on a spit and seafood is grilled over apple wood or roasted in the wood oven. Appetizers are particularly imaginative. Entrées begin around $20. The restaurant is a joint project with Street and Company owner Dana Street.

Arts District

These restaurants are clustered from Danforth Street (an area sometimes referred to as the Studio District) up to and around Congress Street. If you feel like just browsing and finding a spot, walk Congress Street, from around Longfellow Square down to Congress Square, for an ever-evolving variety of ethnic

and mainstream choices. Be sure to ask about renowned chef Erik Desjarlais's planned new restaurant **Evangeline** (190 State St.) on Longfellow Square. Expected are both three-course a-la-carte and seven-to-fifteen-course degustation menus, bar and table seating, a well-chosen wine menu, and artwork on view.

Local Flavors: Even the name **Norm's Bar and Grill** (617 Congress St., 207/828-9944, 11:30 A.M.–10 P.M., opens at 4 P.M. Sun.) is reminiscent of *Cheers*. Locals would prefer this neighborhood eatery were kept secret, but the food is too good not to share. One of the reasons Norm's is so popular is that you can cobble together a meal that meets your appetite from a menu that includes selections for tapas, sandwiches, salads, entrées, and sides in addition to chalkboard specials. Norm's doesn't take reservations, so you'll probably have to relax in the equally popular bar while waiting for a table. Norm also operates the tavern across the street and a barbecue joint in the Old Port.

Ole! Healthful Mexican is served at **Mesa Verde** (618 Congress St., 774-6089, 11:30 A.M.–9 P.M. Tues.–Thurs., to 9:30 P.M. Fri. and Sat., to 8:30 P.M. Sun.), a colorful restaurant and juice bar that also is rightfully famous for its margaritas.

If your sweet tooth is calling, answer it at **geo's patisserie café** (27 Forest Ave., 207/699-2665, www.geospatisserie.com, 7 A.M.–6 P.M. Mon.–Fri., 8 A.M.–5 P.M. Sat.), a European-style scratch bakery where chef George Gilfoil creates delicious pastries and also serves lunch.

Can't make up your mind? Peruse the choices available at **Public Market House** (28 Monument Sq., 207/228-2056, http://publicmarkethouse.com, 8 A.M.–6 P.M. Mon.–Fri., 9 A.M.–6 P.M. Sat., 10 A.M.–3 P.M. Sun.), which came about after the closure of the Portland Public Market. This is far smaller, but the quality and the fun are still there. It's a growing space, with maybe a half dozen vendors selling sandwiches, baked goods, soups, and other fresh fare.

Eclectic: Ever-popular **€ Local 188** (685 Congress St., 207/761-7909, www.local188.com,

11 A.M.–3 P.M. and 5:30–10:30 P.M. daily) moved from its funky digs to a larger, more comfortable space, keeping its spirit but maturing (a bit) in decor. This place serves fabulous Mediterranean-inspired food with a tapas-heavy menu. It doubles as an art gallery, with rotating exhibits. Spend lunch, Saturday or Sunday brunch (10 A.M.–3 P.M.), or an evening grazing through marinated mushrooms, vegetable salads, imaginative soups, mussel stew, even paella. Tapas selections are all under $10, heartier choices and entrées run $10–18. Free parking behind the building.

Be sure to have a reservation if you're going, pretheater, to **BiBo's Madd Apple Café** (23 Forest Ave., 207/774-9698, 11:30 A.M.–2 P.M. Wed.–Fri., 5:30–9 P.M. Wed.–Sat., 11 A.M.–2 P.M. and 4–8 P.M. Sun.)—it's right next to the Portland Performing Arts Center. On the other hand, it's popular anytime, thanks to chef Bill Boutwell (BiBo). There's no way of predicting what will be on the bistro-fusion menu, although the sweet soy-marinated salmon is so popular that it's almost always available. Dinner entrée range is $15–25.

Well off most tourists' radar screens is **Artemesia Café** (61 Pleasant St., 207/761-0135, 11 A.M.–3 P.M. Mon.–Fri., 9 A.M.–2 P.M. Sat. and Sun., and from 5 P.M. Thurs.–Sat.), but it's another one of Portland's little surprises. It's a bright spot serving a creative menu that draws upon international influences.

Ethnic Fare: Portland has a number of good Japanese restaurants. **Yosaku** (1 Danforth St., 207/780-0880, 11:30 A.M.–2 P.M. and 5–9:30 P.M. Mon.–Thurs., to 10:30 P.M. Fri. and Sat., to 9 P.M. Sun., and noon–3 P.M. Sat. and Sun.) is an old standby serving delicious sushi along with noodle dishes, tempuras, and other Japanese favorites.

Newer on the scene is **Miyake** (129 Spring St., 207/871-9170, noon–2 P.M. Tues.–Fri., 5–9 P.M. Mon.–Thurs., to 9:30 P.M. Fri. and Sat.), chef Masa Miyake's tiny, ultra informal neighborhood joint, which quickly established itself as a must-go; BYOB. The decor is Pepsi and plastic, but don't let that dissuade you, you can always get it to go.

Destination Dining: Fun, whimsical, and artsy best describes most restaurants in the Arts District, but not **Five Fifty-Five** (555 Congress St., 207/761-0555, www.fivefifty-five.com, 5–10 P.M. Mon.–Thurs., to 10:30 P.M. Fri. and Sat., 10:30 A.M.–2:30 P.M. (brunch) and 5–9:30 P.M. Sun.), where chef Steve Corry was named by *Food and Wine* as one of the top 10 best new chefs in the country. The bilevel dining area is bright and elegant. Fresh, local, and seasonal are blended in creative ways on his ever-changing menu, which is divided into small plates, green plates, savory plates, cheese plates, and sweet plates, with prices ranging about $8–30. A five-course tasting menu is available with 24-hour notice. If you can't afford to splurge in the main restaurant, Corry serves lighter fare in the lounge.

West End

Chef Abby Harmon's **Caiola's Restaurant** (58 Pine St., 207/772-1111, www.caiolas.com, 5:30–9:30 P.M. Tues.–Thurs., to 10 P.M. Fri. and Sat.) delivers a taste of Europe derived from local farms and gardens. It deserves its buzz as far more than a neighborhood spot. Harmon draws upon her experience at some of Maine's top restaurants, and her staff is well trained. Entrées begin around $14.

Superb, thin-crust pizzas in usual and unusual flavor combos emerge from the wood-fired oven at chef Oliver Outerbridge's **Bonobo** (Pine and Bracket Sts., 207/347-8267, 11 A.M.–11 P.M. Mon.–Sat.). After the pizza, head to the ice-cream window, serving Maple's Organics gelato.

Have breakfast or lunch or pick up prepared foods at **Aurora Provisions** (64 Pine St., 207/871-9061, www.auroraprovisions.com, 8 A.M.–6:30 P.M. Mon.–Sat.), a combination market and café with irresistible goodies, most made on the premises.

Tiny **Dogfish Cafe** (953 Congress St., 207/253-5400, 11:30 A.M.–10 P.M. Mon.–Sat.) packs 'em in for salads and sandwiches and grilled goodies, averaging around $10, with heartier dinner specials ($11–18) served evenings Wednesday–Saturday. It's just a couple of doors down from the Inn on St. John.

Bayside

Fine Dining: For an elegant meal, look no farther than the **❰❰ Back Bay Grill** (65 Portland St., near the main post office, 207/772-8833, 5:30–9:30 P.M. Mon.–Thurs., to 10 P.M. Fri. and Sat.). The serene dining room is accented by a colorful mural, and arts-and-crafts wall sconces cast a soft glow on the white linen-draped tables. The menu, which highlights fresh, seasonal ingredients, ranks among the best in the city, and the wine list is long and well chosen. Service is professional. Entrées are $19–35 and worth every penny.

Casual Dining: In-the-know Portlanders have long favored **Bintliff's American Café** (98 Portland St., 207/774-0005, www.bintliffscafe.com, 7 A.M.–2 P.M. daily and 5–9 P.M. Wed.–Sat.) for its fabulous brunches ($7–12); the menu is humongous. It also serves a much smaller dinner menu (entrées $17–25) to equally rave reviews. It takes no reservations for brunch, so expect to wait in line on weekends (it's worth it).

East End

These dining spots are all east of the Franklin Street Arterial, with most concentrated in the food-oriented neighborhood of India and Middle Streets. Poke around this end of the city, and you'll find quite a few ethnic hole-in-the-wall places on and around Washington Avenue. It's an ever-changing array, but if you're adventurous, give one a try.

Local Flavors: The most incredible fries come from **❰❰ Duckfat** (43 Middle St., 207/774-8080, www.duckfat.com, 11 A.M.–8 P.M. Mon.–Thurs., to 9 P.M. Fri. and Sat., noon–6 P.M. Sun.), an ultracasual, order-at-the-counter joint owned by chef Rob Evans (of Hugo's fame), so you know it's not only good, but it has that spark, too. Fries, fried in duck fat, of course, are served in a paper cone and accompanied by your choice of sauce from six options; the truffle ketchup is heavenly. Want to really harden those arteries? Order the *poutine,*

Belgian fries topped with Maine cheese curd and homemade duck gravy. In addition, Duckfat serves paninis, soups, salads, and really good milk shakes; wine and beer are available, too.

Mmmmm, mmmm. For finger-lickin' barbecued ribs and chicken, fried chicken, blackened catfish, and pulled pork or beef brisket sandwiches, it's **Norm's East End Grill** (37 Middle St., 207/253-1700, 11:30 A.M.–10 P.M. Mon.–Sat., 5–9 P.M. Sun.). All barbecue items are smoked on the premises with hickory and apple wood. Of course, this being Maine, clam and corn chowder, homemade fish cakes, and lobster stew are also available.

Mainers love their Italian sandwiches, and **Amato's** (71 India St., 207/773-1682, www.amatos.com, 6:30 A.M.–11 P.M. Mon.–Fri., opens 7 A.M. Sun.) is credited with creating this drool-worthy sub, made with ham, cheese, tomatoes, green peppers, black olives, and onions (or various other combinations), all wrapped in a doughy roll and drizzled with olive oil. Also available are calzones, salads, and other Italian-inspired foods. Amato's has outlets throughout southern Maine. This one has outdoor patio seating.

Micucci's Grocery Store (45 India St., 207/775-1854) has been servicing Portland's Italian community since 1949. It's a great stop for picnic fixings and a nice selection of inexpensive wines. It's also home to baker Stephen Lanzalotta's to-die-for breads and pastries, soups, little pizzas, and other healthful, delicious Mediterranean-style foods.

Huge portions at rock-bottom prices makes **Silly's** (40 Washington Ave., 207/772-0360, www.sillys.com, 11:30 A.M.–9 P.M. Tues.–Sun.) an ever-popular choice among the young and budget minded; it has a huge menu, too, with lots of international flair and milk shakes in dozens of wacko flavors. And the decor? Vintage 1950s Formica and chrome.

It's hard not to like **North Star Cafe** (225 Congress St., 207/699-2994, www.northstarmusiccafe.com, 7 A.M.–10 P.M. Mon.–Wed., to 11 P.M. Thurs.–Sat., 8 A.M.–4 P.M. Sun.), a low-key and comfy coffeehouse serving excellent soups, sandwiches, and salads, most made from locally sourced and organic ingredients. Music or readings occur almost every evening.

Just try *not* to walk out with something from Two **Fat Cats Bakery** (47 India St., 207/347-5144); the cookies! the breads! the pies!

Casual Dining: Blue Spoon (89 Congress St., 207/773-1119, 11 A.M.–3 P.M. and 5–9 P.M. Tues.–Sat.) was one of the first upscale eateries on Portland's gentrifying East End. Chef/owner David Iovino, who studied at the French Culinary Institute, has created a warm, welcoming, and inexpensive bistro (entrées $9–13), where one of the best sellers is roast chicken that's pan seared and then roasted beneath a hot brick. Vegetarian and vegan selections are available.

A more recent addition to the neighborhood is **Bar Lola** (100 Congress St., 207/775-5652, 5–10 P.M. Wed.–Sat.), an intimate and cozy neighborhood bistro serving an all-tapas menu—small portions, big flavors.

Primo rustic Italian fare is the rule at **Ribollita** (41 Middle St., 207/774-2972, 5–9 P.M. Tues.–Thurs., to 10 P.M. Fri. and Sat.). You'll want reservations at this small, casual restaurant that's justly popular for delivering fabulous food at fair prices ($12–20); just be in the mood for a leisurely meal. Handmade pastas, such as white bean and Romano ravioli or pan-seared gnocchi, and choices such as radicchio-wrapped salmon with pesto and roast pepper sauce are typical.

You never know what'll be on the menu (Indonesian chicken, North African stuffed peppers, maybe Caribbean shrimp cakes?) at funky **Pepperclub** (78 Middle St., 207/772-0531, www.pepperclubrestaurant.com, 5–9 P.M. Sun.–Thurs., to 10 P.M. Fri. and Sat.), but take the risk. Vegetarian and vegan specials are always available, as are local and organic meats and seafood. If your kids are even vaguely adventuresome, they'll find food to like here—and prices to match (entrées $11–15). In the mornings, it morphs into **The Good Egg** (7–11 A.M. Mon.–Fri., 8 A.M.–1 P.M. Sat. and Sun.), serving breakfast, including gluten-free foods.

Destination Dining: In 2004, *Food and Wine* named Rob Evans as one of America's 10 Best New Chefs, and in 2007 he was a Beard nominee for Best Chef in the Northeast, making ◖ **Hugo's** (88 Middle St., corner of Franklin St., 207/774-8538, www.hugos.net, 5:30–9 P.M. Tues.–Thurs., to 9:30 P.M. Sat. and Sun.) a destination unto itself. Not that savvy Portlanders hadn't already been beating a path to his door for his outstanding New American cuisine. In 2008, Evans and partner Nancy Pugh planned to change the formal fixed-price, multicourse menu to an à la carte one (most entrées $15–28) and present a more casual face. Evans will still draw from the freshest Maine ingredients available. Bar seating is available; for the dining room, reservations are essential.

The 'Burbs

Great sunset views over Portland's skyline, a casual atmosphere, and excellent fare have earned **Saltwater Grille** (231 Front St., South Portland, 207/799-5400, www.saltwatergrille.com, 11 A.M.–3 P.M. and 5–9 P.M. daily) an excellent reputation. Dine inside or on the waterfront deck. Dinner entrées run $15–25.

How about a four-course lunch, with a matchless view, on the cheap? The students in the hospitality program at Southern Maine Community College (Fort Rd., Spring Point, South Portland) need practice for their cooking and service skills, so their "labs" are two restaurants. During the academic year, the **Culinary Arts Dining Room** serves a four-course lunch Wednesday and Thursday and a buffet Friday noon–1:30 P.M., for $10.50, with reservations; call 207/741-5612.

Pizza: Ricetta's Brick Oven Pizzeria (29 Western Ave., Rte. 9, South Portland, between Maine Mall and Portland Jetport, 207/775-7400, and 240 Rte. 1, Falmouth, 207/781-3100, 11:30 A.M.–10 P.M., to 11 P.M. Fri. and Sat.) is regularly voted Greater Portland's best pizza palace. It's not surprising when you see the lunchtime-only pizza smorgasbord—all the pizza you can eat, plus salad and soup. Specialty pizzas are outstanding, or you can invent your own combo. Also on the menu are antipasti, calzones, giant salads, soups, pasta dishes, and high-calorie desserts.

Lobster in the Rough: Every Mainer has a favorite lobster eatery (besides home), but **The Lobster Shack** (222 Two Lights Rd., Cape Elizabeth, 207/799-1677, www.lobstershack-twolights.com, 11 A.M.–8 P.M. mid-Apr.–mid-Oct.) tops an awful lot of lists. Seniority helps—it's been here since the 1920s. Scenery, too—a panoramic vista in the shadow of Cape Elizabeth Light. Plus the menu—seafood galore (and hot dogs for those who'd rather). Choose a lobster from the tank; indulge in the lobster stew; grab a table on the ledges and watch the world sail by. Opt for a sunny day; the lighthouse's foghorn can kill your conversation when the fog rolls in.

INFORMATION AND SERVICES
Information
The Visitor Information Center of the Convention and Visitors Bureau of Greater Portland (245 Commercial St., Portland 04101, 207/772-4994, www.visitportland.com) has tons of brochures, plenty of restaurant menus, and public restrooms. The Portland Downtown District (94 Free St., 207/772-6828, www.portland-maine.com) has a useful website.

Check out the Portland Public Library (5 Monument Sq., 207/871-1700, www.portlandlibrary.com).

For winter parking-ban information, call 207/879-0300.

Public Restrooms
In the Old Port area, you'll find restrooms at the Convention and Visitors Bureau Visitor Information Center (245 Commercial St.), the Spring Street parking garage (45 Spring St.), the Fore Street Parking Garage (419 Fore St.), and the Casco Bay Lines ferry terminal (Commercial and Franklin Sts.).

On Congress Street, find restrooms at Portland City Hall (389 Congress St.) and the Portland Public Library (5 Monument Sq.). In Midtown, head for the Cumberland County

Civic Center (1 Civic Center Sq.). In the West End, use Maine Medical Center.

GETTING THERE AND AROUND
The best overall source for planning your transportation is the website www.transportme.org. It lists schedules, fares, and other information for airlines, buses, ferries, and trains.

The ultraclean and comfortable Portland Transportation Center (100 Thompson Point Rd., Portland, 207/828-3939) is the base for **Concord Trailways** (800/639-3317, concordtrailways.com) and **Amtrak's Downeaster** (800/872-7245, www.thedowneaster.com). Parking is $3 per day, and the terminal has free coffee, free newspapers (while they last), and vending machines. The **Metro** (114 Valley St., P.O. Box 1097, Portland 04104, 207/774-0351, $1.25 exact change), **The Portland Explorer** (207/774-9891 or 800/377-4457, www.portlandexplorer.org, free), and the Zoom buses, with service from Biddeford/Saco, stop here and connect with **Portland International Jetport** (207/774-7301, www.portlandjetport.org), **Vermont Transit Lines** (950 Congress St., 207/772-6587 or 800/552-8737), and **Casco Bay Lines ferry service** (www.cascobaylines.com). If you show your Trailways or Amtrak ticket stub to the Metro bus driver, you'll have a free ride downtown. Taxis charge $1.40 for the first plus $0.25 for each additional one-ninth mile.

Parking garages and lots are strategically situated all over downtown Portland, particularly in the Old Port and near the civic center. Unless you're lucky, you'll probably waste a lot of time looking for on-street parking (meters start at $0.25 a half hour), so a garage or lot is the best option. If you land in a garage or lot with a Park and Shop sticker, you can collect free-parking stamps, each good for an hour, from participating shops and restaurants. You could even end up parking for free. A day of parking generally runs $8–16. The Casco Bay Lines website (www.cascobaylines.com) has a very useful parking map, listing parking lots and garages and their hourly and daily rates. It's good for comparison shopping.

Freeport

Freeport has a special claim to historic fame—it's the place where Maine parted company from Massachusetts in 1820. The documents were signed on March 15, making Maine its own separate state.

At the height of the local mackerel-packing industry here, countless tons of the bony fish were shipped out of South Freeport, often in ships built on the shores of the Harraseeket River. Splendid relics of the shipbuilders' era still line the streets of South Freeport, and no architecture buff should miss a walk, cycle, or drive through the village. Even downtown Freeport still reflects the shipbuilder's craft, with contemporary shops tucked in and around handsome historic houses. Some have been converted to B&Bs, others are boutiques, and one even disguises the local McDonald's franchise.

Today, Freeport is best known as the mecca for the shop-till-you-drop set. The hub, of course, is sportswear giant L. L. Bean, which has been here since 1912, when founder Leon Leonwood Bean began making his trademark hunting boots (and also unselfishly handed out hot tips on where the fish were biting). More than 120 retail operations now fan out from that epicenter, and you can find almost anything in Freeport (pop. about 7,700)—except maybe a parking spot in midsummer.

When (or if) you tire of shopping, you can always find quiet refuge in the town's preserves and parks—Mast Landing Sanctuary, Wolfe's Neck Woods State Park, and Winslow Memorial Park—and plenty of local color at the Town Wharf in the still honest-to-goodness fishing village of South Freeport.

An orientation note: Don't be surprised to receive directions (particularly for South Freeport) relative to "the Big Indian"—a 40-foot-tall landmark at the junction of Route 1 and South Freeport Road. If you stop at the Maine Visitor Information Center in Yarmouth and continue on Route 1 toward Freeport, you can't miss it, just north of the Freeport Inn and the Casco Bay Inn.

SHOPPING

Logically, this category must come first in any discussion of Freeport, since shopping's the biggest game in town. It's pretty much a given that anyone who visits Freeport intends to darken the door of at least one shop.

❰ L. L. Bean

If it's *only* one, it's likely to be "Bean's." The whole world beats a path to L. L. Bean (95 Main St., Rte. 1, 207/865-4761 or 800/341-4341, www.llbean.com)—or so it seems in July, August, and December. Established as a hunting/fishing supply shop, this giant sports outfitter now sells everything from kids' clothing to cookware on its ever-expanding downtown campus. In 2007, it moved the hunting and fishing store into the expanded main store, and in 2008, the outlet store—a great source for deals on equipment and clothing—moved into the former hunting and fishing building, behind the main store. It's also partnered on a new parking and retail facility, expected to open in 2009, with as many as 40 shops. It's under construction on land behind Bow and Main Streets.

By 2010, Bean's aspires to have a new outdoor adventure center in full operation on its 700-acre property on Desert Road. Possibilities include a restaurant, lodging, a golf course, and opportunities for extended stay and participation packages for sports in its Walk-On Adventures and other programs, such as kayaking, canoeing, cross-country skiing, snowshoeing, shooting, and archery. Some opportunities may open prior to 2010.

Until the 1970s, Bean's remained a rustic store with a creaky staircase and a closet-size women's department. Then a few other merchants began arriving, Bean's expanded, and a feeding frenzy followed. The Bean reputation rests on a savvy staff, high quality, an admirable environmental consciousness, and a no-questions-asked return policy. Bring the kids—for the indoor trout pond, the clean re-

MAINE WILDLIFE PARK

If you want to see where Maine's wild things are, venture a bit inland to visit the Maine Wildlife Park (Shaker Rd./Rte. 26, Gray, 207/657-4977, 9:30 A.M.-6 P.M. daily, gate closes 4:30 P.M. mid-Apr.-Veterans' Day, $6 ages 13-60, $4.50 seniors, $4 kids 4-12). Nearly 25 native species of wildlife can be seen at this state-operated wildlife refuge, including such ever-popular species as moose, black bear, white-tailed deer, and bald eagle. The park began in 1931 as a state-run game farm. For more than 50 years, the Department of Inland Fish and Game reared pheasants here for release during bird-hunting season. At the same time, wildlife biologists and game wardens with the state's Department of Inland Fisheries and Wildlife needed a place to care for orphaned or injured animals.

In 1982, the farm's mission was changed to that of a wildlife and conservation education facility. Today the park is a temporary haven for wildlife, but those who cannot survive in the wild live here permanently.

Among the wildlife that have been in residence at the park are lynx, deer, opossum, black bear, bobcat, porcupine, raccoon, red-tailed hawk, barred and great horned owl, mountain lion, bald eagle, raven, skunk, woodchuck, and coyote. Other frequent guests include wild turkey, fisher, gray fox, kestrel, turkey vulture, wood turtle, and box turtle. Most are here for protection and healing, and while they're in residence, visitors are able to view them at close range.

In addition to the wildlife, there are numerous interactive exhibits and displays to view, nature trails to explore, a nature store, snack shack, and even picnic facilities. Special programs and exhibits are often offered on weekends mid-May-mid-September.

The park is 3.5 miles north of downtown Gray and Maine Turnpike Exit 63. From the coast, take Route 115 from Main Street in downtown Yarmouth, continuing through North Yarmouth (with stunning old houses) to Gray, and then head north on Route 26 for 3.5 miles.

strooms, and the "real deal" outlet store. The store's open-round-the-clock policy has become its signature, and if you show up at 2 A.M., you'll have much of the store to yourself, and you may even spy vacationing celebrities or the rock stars who often visit after Portland shows.

Outlets and Specialty Stores

After Bean's, it's up to your whims and your wallet. The stores stretch for several miles up and down Main Street and along many side streets. Pick up a copy of the *Official Map and Visitor Guide* at any of the shops or restaurants, at one of the visitor kiosks, or at the Hose Tower Information Center (23 Depot St., two blocks east of L. L. Bean). All the big names are here, as are plenty of little ones. Don't overlook the small shops tucked on the side streets, such as **Earrings and Company, Wilbur's of Maine Chocolate Confections,** and **Edgecomb Potters.**

PARKS, PRESERVES, AND OTHER ATTRACTIONS
Mast Landing Sanctuary

More than two miles of easy, yellow-blazed trails wind through the 140-acre Mast Landing Sanctuary, an area that ages ago was the source of masts for the Royal Navy. Pick up a trail map at the parking area and start watching for birds. The best (and longest) route is the 1.6-mile Loop Trail, which passes fruit trees, hardwoods, and an old milldam. (Keep the kids off the dam.) Maine Audubon owns the sanctuary. The society operates a very popular nature day camp here late June–mid-August each summer; call for the schedule. The sanctuary is open sunrise–sunset, year-round, and is popular in winter with cross-country skiers. Admission is free. From downtown Freeport (Rte. 1), take Bow Street (opposite L. L. Bean) one mile east to Upper Mast Landing Road. Turn left (north) and go 500 feet to the parking area.

Wolfe's Neck Woods State Park

Five miles of easy to moderate trails meander through 233-acre Wolfe's Neck Woods State Park (Wolfe's Neck Rd., 207/865-4465, $3 ages 11–64, $1 children 5–11), just a few minutes' cycle or drive from downtown Freeport. You'll need a trail map, available near the parking area. The easiest route (partly wheelchair-accessible) is the Shoreline Walk, about three-quarters of a mile, starting near the salt marsh and skirting Casco Bay. Sprinkled along the trails are helpful interpretive panels explaining various points of natural history—bog life, osprey nesting, glaciation, erosion, and tree decay. Guided tours are offered at 2 P.M. daily mid-July–late August, weather permitting. Leashed pets are allowed. Adjacent **Googins Island,** an osprey sanctuary, is off-limits. From downtown Freeport, follow Bow Street (across from L. L. Bean) for 2.25 miles; turn right onto Wolfe's Neck Road (also called Wolf Neck Rd.) and go another 2.25 miles.

Wolfe's Neck Farm

The best time to visit Wolfe's Neck Farm (10 Burnett Rd., 207/865-4469, www.wolfesneckfarm.org) is March and April for the annual **Calf Watch,** when about 60 calves and 15 lambs join the herd on the 620-acre farm. During calving season, the farm is open 9 A.M.–5 P.M. daily, and kids can see the latest newborns as well as chickens, turkeys, pigs, and other creatures. Sustainable agriculture and environmental sensitivity are the overriding philosophies at this working farm owned and operated by the nonprofit Wolfe's Neck Farm Foundation. Nature trails lace the property, and a small retail shop in the farmhouse (open 9 A.M.–4:30 P.M. weekdays) sells naturally raised beef, lamb, pork, and eggs.

Winslow Memorial Park

Owned by the town of Freeport, Winslow Memorial Park (Staples Point, South Freeport, 207/865-4198, late May–late Sept., $1.50) is a spectacular 90-plus-acre seaside park, overlooking the islands of upper Casco Bay. Swim off the beach (changing house, restrooms, but no lifeguards), picnic on the shore, walk the three-quarters-mile nature trail and perch on the point, launch a canoe or kayak, or reserve one of the 100 inland or waterfront campsites ($22–29, no hookups, but some sites can take RVs). The boat landing and beach area are tidal, so boaters and swimmers should plan to be here two hours before and two hours after high tide; otherwise, you're dealing with mudflats. From the Big Indian on Route 1, take South Freeport Road one mile to Staples Point Road and continue to the end.

Bradbury Mountain State Park

Six miles from the hubbub of Freeport and you're in tranquil, wooded, 590-acre Bradbury Mountain State Park (Rte. 9, Pownal, 207/688-4712, $3 adults, $1 children 5–11), with facilities for picnicking, hiking, mountain biking, and rustic camping, but no swimming. Pick up a trail map at the gate and take the easy, 0.4-mile (round-trip) Mountain Trail to the 485-foot summit, with superb views east to the ocean and southeast to Portland. In fall, it's gorgeous. Or take the Tote Road Trail, on the western side of the park, where the ghost of Samuel Bradbury occasionally brings a chill to hikers in a hemlock grove. A playground keeps the littlest tykes happy. The nonresident camping fee is $14 per site per night ($11 for residents). The park season is May 15–October 15, but there's winter access for cross-country skiing. From Route 1, cross over I-95 at Exit 20 and continue west on Pownal Road to Route 9.

Pineland Farms

Once a home to Maine's mentally disabled citizens, 1,600-acre Pineland (15 Farm View Dr., New Gloucester, 207/688-4539, www.pinelandfarms.org) campus was closed in 1996. In 2000, the Libra Foundation bought it, and now the property comprises 19 buildings and 5,000 acres of farmland, and much of it is open for recreation. Walk or ski the trails, sight birds in the fields and woods, stroll through the garden, fish the pond or skate on it in winter,

© TOM NANGLE

Glaciers contributed to the formation of the Desert of Maine.

play tennis, go mountain biking or orienteering, or even take a horseback-riding lesson. It's a vast outdoor playground, but your first stop should be the visitors center (9 A.M.–5 P.M. daily) to see a list of any events (frequent ones include guided farm tours and family experiences), pick up maps, pay any necessary fees, shop for farm-fresh products, or even grab lunch or snacks at Foley's Bakery Coffee House or the Commons Caféteria. (Some activities, such as cross-country mountain-biking trail access and horseback-riding lessons require fees.) Also on the premises are a variety of accommodations, with rates beginning at $325–400 per night. No dogs.

Desert of Maine

Okay, so maybe it's a bit hokey, but talk about sands of time. More than 10,000 years ago, glaciers covered the region surrounding the Desert of Maine (95 Desert Rd., 207/865-6962, www.desertofmaine.com, early May–mid-Oct., $8.75 adults, $6.25 ages 13–16, $5.25 ages 6–12). When they receded,

they scoured the landscape, pulverizing rocks and leaving behind a sandy residue that was covered by a thin layer of topsoil. Jump forward to 1797, when William Tuttle bought 300 acres and moved his family here, as well as his house and barn, and cleared the land. Now jump forward again to the present and tour where a once-promising farmland has become a desert wasteland. The guided, safari-style tram tours combine history, geology, and environmental science and an opportunity for children to hunt for "gems" in the sand. Decide for yourself: Is the desert a natural phenomenon? A man-made disaster? Or does the truth lie somewhere in the middle?

Harrington House and Pettengill Farm

A block south of L. L. Bean is the Harrington House (45 Main St., Rte. 1, 207/865-3170, www.freeporthistoricalsociety.org, 10 A.M.–2:30 P.M. Tues., Thurs., and Fri. and 10 A.M.–7 P.M. Wed., free) home base of the Freeport Historical Society. You can pick up walking maps detailing Freeport's architecture for a small fee and tour the house. Exhibits pertaining to Freeport's history and occasionally ones by local artists are presented in two rooms in the restored 1830 Enoch Harrington House, a National Historic Register property.

Also listed on the register is the society's Pettengill Farm, a 19th-century saltwater farm comprising a circa 1810 saltbox-style house, woods, orchards, salt marsh, and lovely perennial gardens. The farmhouse is open only during the annual Pettengill Farm Days in the fall, but the grounds are open at all times. From Main Street, take Bow Street and go 1.5 miles. Turn right onto Pettengill road. Park at the gate, and then walk along the dirt road for about 15 minutes to the farmhouse.

RECREATION AND SPORTS
◖ L. L. Bean Outdoor Discovery Schools
Since the early 1980s, the sports outfitter's Outdoor Discovery Schools (888/552-3261, www.llbean.com) have trained thousands of outdoors enthusiasts to improve their skills in fly-fishing, archery, hiking, canoeing, sea kayaking, winter camping, cross-country skiing, orienteering, and even outdoor photography. Here's a deal that requires no planning. **Walk-On Adventures** provides 1.5–2.5-hour lessons in sports such as kayak touring, fly casting, archery, clay shooting, snowshoeing, and cross-country skiing for $15, including equipment. All of the longer fee programs, plus canoeing and camping trips, require preregistration, well in advance because of their popularity. Some are held in the mountains and on the rivers of western Maine, others are in Maryland and Virginia. Some of the lectures, seminars, and demonstrations held in Freeport are free, and a regular catalog lists the schedule. Bean's waterfront **Flying Point Paddling Center** hosts many of the kayaking, saltwater fly-fishing, and guiding programs and is home to the annual **PaddleSports Festival** in June, with free demonstrations, seminars, vendors, lessons, and more.

◖ Atlantic Seal Cruises
Atlantic Seal Cruises (Town Wharf, South Freeport, 207/865-6112 or 877/285-7325), owned and operated by Captain Tom Ring, makes two or three 2.5-hour cruises daily to 17-acre **Eagle Island,** a State Historic Site once owned by Admiral Robert Peary of North Pole fame. The trip includes a lobstering demonstration (except Sun., when lobstering is banned). Fee is $28 adult, $20 ages 5–12, $15 ages 1–4. Captain Ring also does daylong excursions once a week to **Seguin Island,** off the Phippsburg Peninsula, where you can climb the light tower and see Maine's only first-order Fresnel lens, the largest on the coast. (This trip, which costs $50 adult, $34 under 12, is not for the unsteady; you'll be offloaded from a small boat.) A Seal and Osprey Watch cruise is offered at twilight.

Kayak and Canoe Rentals
Ring's Marine Service (Smelt Brook Rd., South Freeport, 207/865-6143 or 866/865-6143, www.ringsmarineservice.com) rents single kayaks for $38, tandems for $60, and canoes for $28 per day, with longer-term rentals available.

ENTERTAINMENT
Shopping seems to be more than enough entertainment for most of Freeport's visitors, but don't miss the **L. L. Bean Summer Concert Series** (800/341-4341, ext. 37222). At 7:30 P.M. each Saturday early July–Labor Day weekend,, Bean's hosts free big-name, family-oriented events in Discovery Park, in the Bean's complex. Arrive early (these concerts are *very* popular) and bring a blanket or a folding chair. Call for more info.

ACCOMMODATIONS
If you'd prefer to drop where you shop, Freeport has a large country inn, several motels, and more than two dozen B&Bs, so finding a pillow is seldom a problem, but it's still wise to have reservations. For camping, try Winslow Memorial Park and Wolfe's Neck Farm.

© TOM NANGLE

Cruise to Eagle Island to the home Arctic explorer Admiral Peary built to resemble the prow of a ship.

Downtown

One of Freeport's pioneering B&Bs is on the main drag yet away from much of the traffic, in a restored house where Arctic explorer Admiral Donald MacMillan once lived. The 19th-century **White Cedar Inn** (178 Main St., Freeport, 207/865-9099 or 800/853-1269, www.whitecedarinn.com, $145–200) has seven attractive guest rooms with antiques, air-conditioning, and Wi-Fi; some have gas fireplaces; one has a TV and accepts dogs ($20). The full breakfast will definitely power you through a day of shopping.

Two blocks north of L. L. Bean, the **Harraseeket Inn** (162 Main St., Freeport, 207/865-9377 or 800/342-6423, www.harraseeketinn.com, $199–305 peak) is a splendid 84-room country inn with an indoor pool, cable TV, air-conditioning, phones, and Wi-Fi; many rooms have fireplaces and hot tubs. A few rooms are decorated with Thomas Moser furnishings, otherwise decor is colonial reproduction in the two antique buildings and

a modern addition. Rates include a hot-and-cold buffet breakfast and afternoon tea—a refreshing break from power shopping—with finger sandwiches and sweets. Pets are permitted in some rooms. The $25/night fee includes a dog bed, small can of food, treat, and dishes. Ask about packages, which offer excellent value. Children 12 and younger stay free. If you're traveling solo, the nightly Innkeeper's Table (reservation required by 5:30 P.M. for 6:30 P.M. seating, 207/865-1085) is a communal table hosted by an innkeeper and a great way to meet other guests.

Three blocks south of L. L. Bean, on a quiet side street shared with a couple of other B&Bs, is **The James Place Inn** (11 Holbrook St., Freeport, 207/865-4486 or 800/964-9086, www.jamesplaceinn.com, $155–185 peak). Innkeepers Robin and Tori Baron welcome guests to seven comfortable rooms, all with air-conditioning, Wi-Fi, and TV, a few with double whirlpool tubs, and one with a woodburning fireplace and private deck. If the weather's fine, enjoy breakfast on the deck. After shopping, collapse on the hammock for two.

Beyond Downtown

Here's a throwback. Three miles north of downtown is the **Maine Idyll** (1411 Rte. 1, 207/865-4201, www.maineidyll.com, $59–103), a tidy cottage colony operated by the Marstaller family for three generations. Twenty studio to three-bedroom pine-paneled cottages are tucked under the trees. All have refrigerators, fireplaces, and TV, and most have limited cooking facilities. Wi-Fi is available near the office. A light breakfast is included. There are two children's play sets, and well-behaved pets are $4.

The family-run **Casco Bay Inn** (107 Rte. 1, Freeport, 207/865-4925 or 800/570-4970, www.cascobayinn.com, $99–119 peak) is a bit fancier than most motels. It has a pine-paneled lounge with fieldstone fireplace and guest Internet station, with Wi-Fi throughout. The spacious rooms have double sinks in the bath area, and some have a refrigerator and microwave. A continental breakfast with newspaper is included.

Ooohh, and here's a find, if you're lucky enough to snag it, given there's only one guest room. **Wolf Neck Bed and Breakfast** (93 Birch Point Rd., Freeport, 207/865-1725, www.wolfneckbb.com, $175) is Dianne Gaudet and Steve Norton's waterfront, newly built Shingle-style home with one guest suite, complete with sitting room and private deck. Longtime area residents, they're a great resource on the region. They also provide a full breakfast. Bring your own boat and launch it right here or rent a canoe or kayaks from the hosts.

Captain Tom Ring, of Atlantic Seal Cruises, also operates **Atlantic Seal B&B** (25 Main St., South Freeport, 207/865-6112 or 877/285-7325, $150–225) in his mid-19th-century Cape-style home on the harbor. The views are stupendous, and the house is chock-full of antiques and fascinating maritime collectibles; Tom's seafaring Maine roots go back for generations. Despite the heritage, rooms have modern amenities, including air-conditioning and private baths (one detached). Tom whips up a bountiful breakfast, and the location is just steps from Harraseeket Lunch and Lobster. Note: Tom is a technophobe and has neither a computer or answerphone.

Camping

Recompence Shore Campsites (134 Burnett Rd., Freeport, 207/865-9307, www.freeportcamping.com, $21–32) is part of Wolfe's Neck Farm. It's an eco-sensitive campground with 175 wooded tent sites (a few hookups are available), many on the farm's three-mile-long Casco Bay shorefront. For anyone seeking peace, quiet, and low-tech camping in a spectacular setting, this is it. Amenities include a laundry and Wi-Fi. Ice, firewood, ice cream, and snacks are available at the camp store. Quiet, leashed, attended pets are welcome. Quiet time begins at 10 P.M. Swimming depends on the tides; check the tide calendar in a local newspaper. Take Bow Street (across from L. L. Bean) to Wolfe's Neck Road, turn right, and go 1.6 miles to Burnett Road, a left turn.

FOOD

Freeport has an ever-increasing number of places to eat, but nowhere enough to satisfy hungry crowds at peak dining hours on busy days. Go early or late for lunch, and make reservations for dinner.

Local Flavors

South of downtown, **Royal River Natural Foods** (443 Rte. 1, Freeport, 207/865-0046, www.rrnf.com) has a small selection of prepared foods, including soups, salads, and sandwiches, and a seating area.

Craving a proper British tea? **Jacqueline's Tea Room** (201 Main St., Freeport, 207/865-2123, www.jacquelinestearoom.com, 10:30 A.M.–3 P.M.) serves a four-course tea by reservation for $20 pp in an elegant setting. Seatings for the two-hour indulgence are between 11 A.M. and 1 P.M. Tuesday–Friday and every other weekend.

At the Big Indian **Old World Gourmet Deli and Wine Shop** (117 Rte. 1, Freeport, 207/865-4477), the offerings are just as advertised, with sandwiches, soups, salads, and prepared foods. There are a few tables inside, but it's mostly a to-go place.

Casual Dining

The Harraseeket Inn's woodsy-themed ◖ **Broad Arrow Tavern** (162 Main St., 207/865-9377 or 800/342-6423, 11:30 A.M.– 10 P.M., to 11 P.M. Fri. and Sat.), just two blocks north of L. L. Bean but seemingly a world away, is a perfect place to escape shopping crowds and madness. The food is terrific, with everything made from organic and naturally raised foods; prices run $10–23. Can't decide? Opt for the extensive, all-you-can-eat lunch buffet ($17) that highlights a bit of everything.

Good wine and fine martinis are what reels them into **Conundrum** (117 Rte. 1, Freeport, 207/865-0303, 4:30–10 P.M. Tues.–Sat.), near Freeport's Big Indian, but the food is worth noting, too. Dozens of wines by the glass, more than 20 martinis, and 20 champagnes will keep most oenophiles happy. The food, varying from pâtés and cheese platters to cheeseburgers and maple-barbecued chicken, helps keep them sober.

Ethnic Fare

Dine indoors or out on the tree-shaded patio at **Azure Italian Café** (123 Main St., 207/865-123, www.azurecafe.com, 11 A.M.–8 P.M., to 9 P.M. Fri. and Sat.). Go light, mixing selections from antipasto, *insalate,* and *zuppa* choices or savor the heartier entrées ($13–30), such as lasagna *formaggio,* Maine seafood risotto, or lemon-and-thyme roast chicken. The service is pleasant and the indoor dining areas are accented by well-chosen contemporary Maine artwork. Live jazz is a highlight some evenings.

Down the side street across from Azure is **Mediterranean Grill** (10 School St., Freeport, 207/865-1688, www.mediterraneangrill.biz, 11 A.M.–10 P.M. daily). Because it's off Main Street, the Cigri family's excellent Turkish-Mediterranean restaurant rarely gets the crowds. House specialties such as moussaka, lamb chops, and *tiropetes* augment a full range of kebab and vegetarian choices. Or simply make a meal of the appetizers—the platters are meals in themselves. Sandwiches and wraps are available at lunch. Entrées go for $16–25. Dine inside or on the streetside deck.

Two surprisingly good, easy-on-the-budget Asian restaurants share a building on the south end of town. **China Rose** (23 Main St., 207/865-6886, 11 A.M.–9:30 P.M., to 10 P.M. Fri. and Sat.) serves Szechuan, Mandarin, and Hunan specialties in a pleasant first-floor dining area. Upstairs is **Miyako** (207/865-6888, same hours), with an extensive sushi bar menu and it also serves other Japanese specialties, including tempura, teriyaki, *nabemono,* and noodle dishes. Luncheon specials are available at both.

Good food and attentive service has made **Thai Garden** (491 Rte. 1, Freeport, 207/865-6005, 11 A.M.–9 P.M. daily) an ever popular choice for Thai.

Fine Dining

Priciest and worth every penny is the Harraseeket Inn's cloth-and-candles **Maine Dining Room** (207/865-1085, 6–9 P.M., to 9:30 P.M. Fri. and Sat.). The service is excellent, and chef Theda Lyden's commitment to natural and organic foods is impressive. Tableside preparations (for 2–7), such as Caesar salad, chateaubriand, and flaming desserts, add an understated note of theater. Dinner entrées are $24–38. Brunch (11:45 A.M.–2 P.M. Sun., $24.95) is a seemingly endless buffet, with whole poached salmon and Belgian waffles among the highlights.

Lobster

In South Freeport, order lobster in the rough at **Harraseeket Lunch and Lobster Company** (36 Main St., Town Wharf, South Freeport, 207/865-4888, 11 A.M.–8:45 P.M. daily summer hours, closes at 7:45 P.M. spring and fall). Grab a waterfront picnic table, place your order, and go at it. (There's also inside dining.)

GREATER PORTLAND

Be prepared for a wait in midsummer. Fried clams are particularly good here, and they're prepared either breaded or battered. Order both and decide for yourself which is better. Another option: If you're camping nearby, call ahead and order boiled lobsters to go. BYOB; no credit cards.

INFORMATION AND SERVICES

Freeport Merchants Association (Hose Tower, 23 Depot St., Freeport 04032, 207/865-1212 or 800/865-1994, www.freeportusa.com) produces an invaluable foldout map/guide showing locations of all the shops, plus sites of lodgings, restaurants, visitor kiosks, pay phones, restrooms, and car and bike parking. If you're serious about "doing" Freeport, send for one of these guides before you arrive so you can plan your attack and hit the ground running.

Just south of Freeport is the Maine Visitor Information Center (Rte. 1, at I-95 Exit 17, Yarmouth, 207/846-0833), part of the statewide tourism-information network. Staffers are particularly attuned to Freeport and Yarmouth, but the center has brochures and maps for the entire state. Also here are restrooms, phones, picnic tables, vending machines, and a dog-walking area.

MOON MAINE'S SOUTHERN COAST
Avalon Travel
a member of the Perseus Books Group
1700 Fourth Street
Berkeley, CA 94710, USA
www.moon.com

Editor and Series Manager: Kathryn Ettinger
Copy Editor: Karen Gaynor Bleske
Graphics Coordinator: Stefano Boni
Production Coordinators: Amber Pirker,
 Tabitha Lahr
Cover Designer: Nicole Schultz
Map Editor: Kevin Anglin
Cartographers: Kat Bennett, Chris Markiewicz
Proofreader: Jamie Andrade

ISBN-10: 1-59880-259-3
ISBN-13: 978-1-59880-259-7

ABOUT THE AUTHOR

Hilary Nangle

Perhaps it's because she was born under the sign of Aquarius, but Hilary Nangle has always had a passion for the coast. The ocean has been a constant in her life since she first watched the sun rise out of the Atlantic while waiting for the school bus in Cape Elizabeth.

In college, Hilary discovered her love for writing. She briefly pursued a graduate degree in Middle East studies, but when she realized her intended career path would take her far from Maine, she dropped out and became a ski and whitewater-rafting bum. That introduced her to the state's back roads and ignited her sense of wanderlust. When she tired of her parents asking when she was going to get a real job, she drew on her writing skills, working as an editor for the pro ski tour, managing editor for a food trade publication, features editor for a daily newspaper, and as a freelance writer/editor.

Hilary never tires of exploring Maine, always seeking out the off-beat and quirky. To her husband's dismay, she inherited her grandmother's shopping gene and can't pass a used bookstore, artisans' gallery, or antiques shop without browsing. She's equally curious about food and has never met a lobster she didn't like. Hilary still divides her year between the coast and the mountains, residing with her husband, photographer Tom Nangle, and an oversized dog, Bernie, both of whom share her passions for long walks and Maine-made ice cream. To learn more about Hilary, please visit her website, www.HilaryNangle.com.